son; a free Ne[gro]
who was burned [...]
judge, Luke Edw[...]
slavery friend, Re[v...]
a courageous busine[ss...]
man; and a heavy-drinking Illinois
Attorney General, U. F. Linder.

The conclusions at the end of the
book are straightforward and deeply
significant for our time. *Lovejoy:
Martyr to Freedom* will stir the reader.

THE AUTHOR

Paul Simon first achieved recognition
through his Troy newspaper in fighting organized crime in his county.
During this time he appeared as a witness before the Kefauver Committee
and was the subject of a feature story
in *Newsweek* magazine.

Simon bought the paper in Troy
when he was 19, at that time the
youngest newspaper publisher in the
country. Prior to this he attended the
University of Oregon and Dana College in Blair, Nebr.

During his Army service he served
as a special agent for the Counter In-
telligence Corps along the Iron Cur-
tain in central Europe.

Simon has studied political and
economic conditions in more than 80
countries on five continents.

He is completing a book on Lincoln's four terms in the Illinois House
of Representatives.

In 1957 the American Political
Science Association gave him a special
award for "distinguished reporting of
state and local government" for a col-
umn he writes during legislative ses-
sions for more than 300 newspapers.

Simon is serving his first term in
the Illinois Senate after four terms in
the House. Each of his four House
terms he received the Independent
Voters of Illinois "best legislator"
award.

He and his wife, the former Jeanne
Hurley, are the parents of a daughter,
Sheila, and a son, Martin. They live
at Troy, Illinois.

LOVEJOY: MARTYR TO FREEDOM

LOVEJOY
MARTYR TO FREEDOM

By

PAUL SIMON

SAINT LOUIS, MISSOURI

Concordia

Concordia Publishing House, St. Louis, Missouri
Concordia Publishing House Ltd., London, W. C. 1
© 1964 Concordia Publishing House
Library of Congress Catalog Card No. 64-19896
MANUFACTURED IN THE UNITED STATES OF AMERICA

Dedicated to My Brother, the Rev. Arthur Simon, Who Works Among Those in New York City Who Do Not Have Freedom from Want.

Elijah Lovejoy Would Have Appreciated Such Service.

CONTENTS

INTRODUCTION

Few men accomplish much during the course of their lives. They eat, they sleep, they do what society expects of them, but few others are enriched because their feet are on the earth.

This book is the fascinating story of a man who lived less than 35 years — and changed history.

How he did that is related in this book.

Why he did it, I hope, will not be clouded by the stormy facts which cross the pages.

Lovejoy did it because he loved God and man in a way that had meaning in his life. A syrupy, smooth, comfortable "Christianity," which called for no more sacrifice than a Sunday morning collection, was not for him. His was the Christianity of the Christ, a faith that believed in the forgiveness of sins and recognized the necessity of the cross in his personal life. His was a faith that marched.

His was also a life that showed faith in all freedom, not only in the freedoms already achieved. He was willing to die for his religious faith as well as faith in the rightness of the cause of freedom — freedom of the press and freedom for those with dark skins.

His is not the story of a perfect man. You will see his weakness as well as his strength. But, like the prophets of old, Lovejoy will be remembered for the positive things he accomplished.

I hope that the adults who read this book will enjoy it.

I hope that the young people will be moved by this man, Elijah Lovejoy.

His was a life of days filled with service, not of years filled with emptiness; a life of heart, not hate; a life of faith, not fear.

I could wish no finer destiny for anyone.

PAUL SIMON

1

FROM MAINE TO THE FRONTIER

Near a little Maine village on November 9, 1802, a boy was born who would be buried on his birthday 35 years later by a few frightened friends.

His name was Elijah Lovejoy, and the village near which he was born was Albion, Me., located about 40 miles inland from the Atlantic Ocean.

You would hardly expect this peaceful little hamlet to produce a man whom people would hate and persecute and finally kill. You would not expect this quiet town to have born in its midst a man whose death would electrify the nation.

His father, born in the year of the Declaration of Independence, was Rev. Daniel Lovejoy, a Congregational minister who also farmed. He was living in a wooden house on land his grandfather cleared when Elijah was born. Here all the Lovejoy children would learn their first strong lessons in what was right and wrong as well as the ABC's. Elijah was the first of nine children. From his father he learned about the decision his father had made as an uneducated 19-year-old farm boy to leave the fields and become a minister. The elder Lovejoy went to a small academy in Massachusetts. He stayed at the home of a Congregational minister who was well known in New England, Rev. Elijah Parish.

Daniel Lovejoy felt deeply indebted to the minister, and when his firstborn son came he named him Elijah Parish. Elijah Parish Lovejoy throughout his life was almost always called "Parish" by his family.

Rev. Daniel Lovejoy was stern in the religious training he gave to the nine children. He did not have the ability, however, to get along with everyone. He had more moods of "ups and downs" than people usually have. Sometimes he became very depressed, and this was sensed by his family as well as by those who heard him preach. Probably because of his moody nature the father in the family received a variety of smaller preaching assignments rather than a lengthy stay at any one congregation. Typical of his assignments were 3 months of missionary work among the Indians and a 12-week period when he furnished "moral and religious instruction to the poor and destitute."

Elijah's mother was in some ways superior to his father. She was emotionally more stable and fully as devoted to Christian living and serving the cause of her faith as was her husband. She had read widely, including some of the more complicated and "heavy" theological books. She was a gentle but powerful force in the intellectual and spiritual growth of the nine Lovejoy children. Her occasional letters to her oldest son would mean much to him in later years when danger was constantly near.

By the time he was four, black-haired and dark-eyed little Elijah could read the Bible, an ability taught him chiefly by his mother. He was soon memorizing hymns and reportedly memorized more than 100 of them. Attendance at the public schools increased his hunger for books, and he read everything he could get at the local library or among his father's theological books.

The two things his youthful friends remembered best about him were that he was an unusually bright student and an unusually good athlete. Five feet nine inches tall and muscular, he combined natural physical ability with something else that makes a good athlete: courage. This quality eventually would make his name famous.

In most respects his youth was a normal one for someone in the new United States. He enjoyed swimming — was the best swimmer in the area — did his share of plowing, and fished with his grandfather.

Shortly before he was 21 he started at Waterville College (now Colby College) in Maine, a small Baptist-supported school. He was immediately recognized as a superior student, and the administration arranged for financial help to permit him to complete his college work. The president thought Lovejoy was a genius.

The religious atmosphere of his childhood continued to influence his college years. A place at which he stayed on a vacation while attending college distressed him. He thought the woman of the household — a relative — "was as little qualified to educate a family as any person I was ever acquainted with." There were several boarders at the place, and he found himself disgusted "by their shocking profanity and intemperance."

During his childhood his parents had stressed the necessity for religious conversion, believing that some singular experience was necessary really to be a Christian. Elijah was already a little on the moody side, and during his college years he was worried because he had not experienced the conversion he so wanted. He continued to read every theological book he could get; but the more he read, the more he wanted the conversion he had learned about at home. A spectacular type of conversion was considered necessary by many in the early 1800s. Because he could not honestly tell anyone of such spiritual lightning hitting him he described his life as "miserable," and his parents were also movingly unhappy.

Letters between Elijah and his parents were mainly religious discussions. A typical letter from his father started out: "I have felt more than usually concerned of late for the salvation of my children." In one letter 21-year-old college student Elijah wrote to his father: "There have been moments even in my short existence, when to have become a nothingness would have been embraced by me. But those were dreadful moments. I cannot describe them. If I know my own heart, I do now *feel* the necessity of resigning myself into the hands of my God, to mould and guide me at His will; tho I dare not say that I am, at present, willing to do it. All that I know and all that I feel is that religion is important, that I do not possess it, and that without it I am miserable indeed."

He wrote poetry to help relieve his mind of his difficulties.

To add to his problems, he fell in love, and the girl would not have him.

At the age of 23 he graduated from Waterville College at the head of his class.

For graduation he wrote a poem, "Inspirations of the Muse." It was not great poetry but much above average for a college valedictorian. There was a spirit of freedom in this poem, in which he described the mind as "free and unshackled as the viewless wind."

But his high scholastic standing gave him little satisfaction. Later he described himself in a poem:

Of all that knew him few but judged him wrong;
He was of silent and unsocial mood:
Unloving and unloved he passed along;
His chosen path with steadfast aim he trod,
Nor asked nor wished applause, save only of his God.

A school year of teaching at the nearby town of China, Maine, was not challenging enough for him. He decided to head westward. This was 51 years after the Declaration of Independence. The State of Illinois was only nine years old.

A combination of adventure, new opportunities, and patriotism prompted those on the eastern seaboard to do what Horace Greeley advised citizens to do in later years: "Go West, Young Man."

At Bath, Maine, 24-year-old Elijah Parish Lovejoy took a boat for Boston. Storms and strong winds prevented a normal, short passage between the two cities, and Lovejoy found himself "sick, sick, sick." The sight of the big and exciting city of Boston made him forget his seasickness. It was his first view of a "big city."

He thought he would earn some money before heading farther westward, but for five days he looked for a job unsuccessfully. Almost out of money, he decided to walk to Illinois!

Walking to Illinois would have been hard enough if he had had money and if the land to be covered were settled. Besides the physically difficult job of walking so many miles there was the question of how he would eat and the peril of attacks by animals, particularly when he was sleeping. In the western portion of his trip there was also the very real possibility that he might meet Indians who, unhappy with the abuse they had taken from the white man, might take revenge on a young white man traveling alone.

Fortunately Lovejoy kept a diary with details of the hardships of his trip. Having come directly from the physically soft life of a teacher, he found that the long hikes gave him much pain. Depressed as he was ordinarily, these aches and pains, the frequent headaches, and the need to keep going with little food made him all the more wretched.

After several weeks he finally reached New York City. He thought he would try to get a job to make a few dollars and to take a rest from his long hiking. The job he finally got consisted in his *walking* around New York City selling newspaper subscriptions.

But this job gave him money only for living. He was not saving any for his trip west. Finally he made contact with the president of the college he had attended, and the president, who thought highly of Lovejoy, took pity on him and lent him some money. Lovejoy wrote in his diary: "May the God of the wretched reward him ten thousand fold."

The money made the rest of the trip easier.

For a time he had to stop in western New York because of malaria, but he recovered quickly. He was able to afford rides on boats and wagons between his walking expeditions.

He finally ended his journey in Hillsboro, Ill., at the home of John Tillson, a friendly Presbyterian who made Lovejoy feel right at home in the big house, the largest in Montgomery County.

But in Hillsboro, Ill., in 1827 there was no demand for a teacher or a college graduate. Illinois had been settled from the south to the north. Chicago was one of the smallest Illinois towns. Finding a place that needed a teacher meant going to the state capital, Vandalia; to the thriving city of Shawnee-town in deep southern Illinois; to the rapidly growing river city of Alton; or to the big frontier town of St. Louis.

St. Louis was only 75 miles from Hillsboro, and for a man who had traveled from Boston this was not much farther to go.

He packed his few belongings and headed for St. Louis.

2

TEACHING AND EDITING IN A ROUGH CITY

Eight years after its founding by the French in 1764 St. Louis had a population of 399 whites and 198 slaves.

In 1821, six years before Lovejoy arrived in St. Louis, Missouri had been admitted to the Union as a slave state. This was the famous "Missouri Compromise," worked out in the U. S. Senate.

Five years before Lovejoy arrived the Missouri Legislature had incorporated St. Louis, a city with a population of 5,600. By the time Lovejoy arrived, late in 1827, the population undoubtedly exceeded 6,000. For the frontier West this was a tremendous population. After all the small villages and the wilderness Lovejoy had been through, St. Louis seemed a huge metropolis.

Fur trade was the big business, although agriculture and river traffic were also major factors in the growth of St. Louis. Lovejoy saw these things, and he saw the influence of many national groups: French, Spanish, English, and Irish, with a few others taking a minor part. He also saw the big stone auction block near the river where slaves were sold, but there is no evidence that this particularly impressed him.

Unlike his native New England, the frontier town of St. Louis was influenced but little by the church. Here he found no Congregational church at all. This fact, plus the rough-and-tumble atmosphere of St. Louis and his doubts about his Christian conversion, meant that religion was for a while not as important in his life as his parents hoped.

But his religious and New England background was still part of him. Many things happening in St. Louis — the drunkenness, the cursing, the open immorality — he disliked and did not want to become a part of.

At this time neither Missouri nor Illinois had public schools, and Lovejoy thought that this would be a good way to make a living and to bring some "good New England culture" to St. Louis. Surprisingly his school was a big success. It did not change the life of St. Louis to any great degree, but he had an influence on a number of young people — and he found himself rather popular, a pleasant experience that he would never have again.

On top of that his school was making money for him. Not only was he able to send some money to his home in Maine, but he was also able to save some money for himself and to live well, according to St. Louis and frontier standards.

In his letters home he wrote of an "abundance of room yet" in St. Louis and the frontier until they have "the civil and religious privileges with which New England is blessed."

His mother — like any mother — was not happy with her oldest son being so far away on the frontier. She had heard many stories about what life was like in St. Louis, and most of the stories were true. That did not seem like a good place for her son, and she wrote: "You say I might have anticipated the time when my children would leave me. So I have. But I cannot see any necessity why they should go so far from me. What special call have you 2,000 miles from your parents?"

Just as he found teaching in the small community in Maine not challenging enough, so after a year of teaching in St. Louis he became dissatisfied. His chance to make a change came after he had run his school for two years; he bought a half interest in the St. Louis *Times* and became the new editor.

This was at a time when editing a newspaper required not only the ability to write but also the ability to fight. Newspaper editors called each other names in print that people today would not use even in conversation. The editors also said exactly what they thought of public officials and other citizens, and it was not uncommon for a newspaper editor to meet an opponent on the street and to end up badly beaten and bruised.

Lovejoy's rival newspaper in St. Louis was the St. Louis *Beacon,* and that newspaper called him a "little animal" and accused him of not paying his employees. Lovejoy replied that the charge was not true and said that the editor of the *Beacon* was "a mere inflated bladder." The Richmond *Enquirer* called Lovejoy a "contemptible parasite."

These were times when men spoke in extremes and when tolerance was rare. As will be seen in more detail in a later chapter, Lovejoy sometimes went along with the spirit of that period and said things which in later years no responsible newspaper would have said. His letters to his family in New England showed this same intolerance. After Andrew Jackson was inaugurated as President, for example, he referred to him as "an adulterer and murderer" who had "fools and knaves for his advisers."

Two prominent men soon would die in a duel because of articles in Lovejoy's newspaper.

The *Times* was mostly concerned with politics and little else. In his second year as editor Lovejoy was taking a strong stand against Congressman Stephen D. Pettis, who was seeking re-election. The *Times* was not kind in its remarks, and Pettis was not kind in his replies. One of the big issues throughout the nation at that time was whether there should be a national bank. President Andrew Jackson opposed it, and Congressman Pettis supported Jackson. It so happened that a brother of the president of the U. S. Bank lived in St. Louis. He was Major Thomas Biddle. In the process of the Congressman's campaign for reelection, what the newspapers were saying — including Lovejoy's *Times* — stirred up the people. This was particularly true of Congressman Pettis and Major Biddle, and soon Congressman Pettis challenged the major to a duel, not an uncommon challenge in those days.

Major Biddle was nearsighted and said he could accept the challenge only if they fought the duel with pistols just five feet from each other!

That is the way it was fought, and Lovejoy — who had helped cause it — wrote the day after the duel: "We regret to add that both gentlemen are dangerously wounded. Major Biddle is shot through the abdomen, the ball lodging within. Mr. Pettis is shot through the side just below the chest, the ball passing through the entire body. We understand that the conduct of both parties on the ground was entirely honorable." He added that both entered the duel with "coolness and courage."

In the next issue Lovejoy reported that both men had died — giving much more space to Major Biddle, whom he had favored in the political quarrel, than to Congressman Pettis.

He praised both men, however, and noted that "both gentlemen suffered the most excruciating pain from the time of their being wounded till their death." He condemned "false notions of honor" which caused the duel and said that he hoped he would "never again witness such a tragedy."

The next issue contained a poem against dueling.

There was little in the *Times* to indicate that Lovejoy in a few years would be famous for his stand against slavery. The "St. Louis Association for the Improvement of the Breed of Horses" was given more attention than the slavery issue.

The advertisements in the *Times* were like those in any

newspaper in a slave state. Slaves were advertised for sale —
and the *Times* office of Lovejoy was even a clearinghouse for
some trade in slaves. Here are some typical advertisements:

FOR SALE — A first rate NEGRO MAN, about 22 years of
age. Apply at this office.

SALE OF NEGROES by Auction at Lane & Co.

FOR SALE — A likely NEGRO WOMAN with six children.
The woman is between 30 and 35 years of age, and the two
oldest children, twins, are between 10 and 11 years old. They
will be sold for CASH. Apply at this office.

WANTED . . . A Negro Boy from 10 to 14 years old for whom
a good price will be given.

FOR SALE — A likely mulatto boy, in his 16th year, accus-
tomed to cooking and sundry other house business, of good
character. For terms enquire of Col. Coleman at the Land
Office.

There were also advertisements for "Negro Clothes," loose-
fitting and coarse materials which the slaves wore.

That the Negro slaves were not as happy as their white
masters liked to pretend was clear from the number of advertisements Lovejoy had for runaway slaves. Here are a few
of them:

$40 Reward. Ran away from the subscriber on the 23rd, a
Negro man named JOHN. He is about 5 feet high, well pro-
portioned, and has a large dent across his nose.

$20 Reward. Ran away on Sunday evening, a bright Mulatto
Man named Claibourne, about 25 years of age, six feet high,
stout made, a very bright Mulatto, his teeth rather broad, has
a down-cast look when spoken to.

[13]

LOVEJOY: MARTYR TO FREEDOM

$20 Reward. Ran away on Thursday, a NEGRO BOY named BOB, about 14 years of age.

In the East, William Lloyd Garrison was stirring up interest in immediate freedom for slaves. Garrison published a newspaper, the *Liberator*, which stimulated more and more discussion of the issue. People like Garrison, who wanted to give full and immediate freedom to the slaves, were known as abolitionists. Some of Lovejoy's family accepted the abolition beliefs, but Lovejoy thought that anyone favoring these ideas was doing a disservice to the country. His brother Joseph displeased him by becoming an agent in Maine for Garrison's newspaper, the *Liberator*.

The American Colonization Society was organized with intentions of sending Negroes back to Africa as free men. This society was composed partially of men who felt that something was wrong with slavery, but who did not feel so moved that they wanted to free all slaves in the United States immediately. Others in the group were not particularly hostile to slavery, but feared the presence of Negroes in their midst, particularly free Negroes. These people felt that sending the Negro back to Africa solved the immediate threat they faced from free Negroes. Some from a desire to free slaves, and some from fear of the Negro, contributed money for the cause. In a sense this group was a compromise between the supporters of slavery and the abolitionists, who opposed slavery.

Lovejoy showed some interest in the St. Louis branch of the American Colonization Society. But slavery was not an important issue to him at that time. More important to him was the consideration whether Jackson or Clay would be President and who would lead the St. Louis political scene.

As a matter of fact, a slave worked in the office of Lovejoy's newspaper.

His name was William — later called William Brown. In

[14]

a few years he escaped to freedom in Canada. After he got his freedom, he wrote a brief autobiography. In it he tells of the days in which he heard his mother whipped and of his gradual growth in slavery. He has a few lines about Lovejoy.

I was soon taken from Mr. Colburn's, and hired to Elijah P. Lovejoy, who was at that time publisher and editor of the "St. Louis Times." My work, while with him, was mainly in the printing office, waiting on the hands, working the press, &c. Mr. Lovejoy was a very good man, and decidedly the best master that I had ever had. I am chiefly indebted to him, and to my employment in the printing office, for what little learning I obtained while in slavery.

While living with Mr. Lovejoy, I was often sent on errands to the office of the "Missouri Republican," published by Mr. Edward Charles. Once, while returning to the office with type, I was attacked by several large boys, sons of slaveholders, who pelted me with snowballs. Having the heavy form of type in my hands, I could not make my escape by running; so I laid down the type and gave them battle. They gathered around me, pelting me with stones and sticks, until they overpowered me, and would have captured me, if I had not resorted to my heels. Upon my retreat, they took possession of the type; and what to do to regain it I could not devise. Knowing Mr. Lovejoy to be a very humane man, I went to the office, and laid the case before him. He told me to remain in the office. He took one of the apprentices with him, and went after the type, and soon returned with it; but on his return informed me that Samuel McKinney had told him that he would whip me, because I had hurt his boy. Soon after, McKinney was seen making his way to the office by one of the printers, who informed me of the fact, and I made my escape through the back door.

McKinney not being able to find me on his arrival, left the office in a great rage, swearing that he would whip me to death. A few days after, as I was walking along Main Street, he seized me by the collar, and struck me over the head five or six times with a large cane, which caused the blood to gush from my nose and ears in such a manner that my clothes were completely saturated with blood. After beating me to his satisfaction, he let me go, and I returned to the office so weak from the loss of blood, that Mr. Lovejoy sent me home to my master. It was five weeks before I was able to walk again. During this time it was necessary to have some one to supply my place at the office, and I lost the situation.

Soon Lovejoy's attitude toward slavery would undergo a radical change that would result in his own death and a shock to the nation.

3

A RELIGIOUS EXPERIENCE

People who knew Lovejoy in St. Louis considered him rather "straitlaced," and many would have been surprised to learn that he belonged to no church.

The influence of a strong Christian home was part of his daily living, but he had never experienced religious conversion in the form that his parents had hoped for and Congregationalism at that time expected.

He was not wealthy, but compared with most of the population he was living well. The comfortable life he was leading did not call for any revolutionary changes.

The St. Louis *Times* did encourage religious activities, whether by a local church or by the new societies that were coming to the frontier to promote Bible reading, tract distribution, Sunday school work, and temperance in drinking. The only group Lovejoy is known to have joined was the Missouri and Illinois Tract Society, of which he became recording secretary.

When a man came to St. Louis to speak against religion, Lovejoy attacked what he had to say.

Lovejoy went to hear various evangelists and religious leaders when they visited St. Louis, but none made any significant dent in his lack of active interest in religion.

We know from his letters home that he went to church regularly. There were also occasional editorial comments that indicated church interest. Once he wrote in his newspaper: "We know not how it may be in the Episcopal and Methodist Churches of the City; but in the Presbyterian Church, the singing is absolutely intolerable." He suggested that the choir's singing might be appreciated more by dogs than by human beings — not a move to make him popular with choir members!

A year after he became editor of the *Times* he attended the revival meetings held in the First Presbyterian Church in St. Louis. A religious revival was "sweeping the country" and in 1831 reached the Western city of St. Louis. These revival services were a series of nightly meetings which he attended regularly. He wrote to his parents that he was praying to be converted, and they joined in that prayer, but at the end of the series of services Lovejoy was not among the converts. It was a great disappointment to his parents and to Lovejoy. More and more he lost interest in religion.

Six months later another series of revival meetings was held at the same church. The guest speaker was Rev. David Nelson — called Dr. Nelson — who was regarded as one of the ablest speakers on the Western frontier. This was in January, and men, women, and children crowded into the warm church from the cold outdoors and in candlelight heard Dr. Nelson condemn sin with vigor. As members of a frontier society the people who gathered in front of Dr. Nelson understood what he was talking about. In clear pictures he showed them what they were doing.

This minister not only attacked sin in a general way but also pinpointed it. One of the sins he brought to life before his hushed audiences was slavery. He made them see that the sale of human beings that was taking place in their city and state was condemned by God. For one man to own another man was, in the eyes of God, a sin as great as adultery or murder.

Those who heard Dr. Nelson were greatly moved. During this series of revivals there were more than twice as many converts as during the revival services the previous year. One of the converts was Elijah Parish Lovejoy.

Most of us who read his letters and writings today would regard Lovejoy as already a Christian and his "conversion" more of a dedication to greater religious practice. He clearly accepted the traditional Christian beliefs although he had not had the emotional experience many expected.

Lovejoy did not regard himself as a Christian until this "conversion" took place.

Whether it is called a conversion or a dedication, it had a profound effect on his life — and finally on the national life. Dr. Nelson certainly had no idea of what he was doing to either the man or the nation when he noted that among his converts at the First Presbyterian Church was a young newspaper editor named Lovejoy.

Lovejoy wrote to his parents to tell them of his conversion, and they were tremendously pleased. His mother said it was "just what I have prayed for with all my heart." It was particularly meaningful to his mother because one of Elijah's younger brothers, Daniel, had died unexpectedly. His mother said Daniel's death "overwhelmed me with gloom and despondency." His father was also pleased, but said that Elijah praised his parents too much for giving him a religious background. "You give us more credit than we think we deserve," he wrote.

At that time and at that place conversion usually meant more than simply a statement of faith and attending church services with greater regularity. It meant changing the whole direction of life. It included an agreement to do your share in changing the lives of others.

The local minister of the First Presbyterian Church was Rev. William Potts. Lovejoy was uncertain what he must do, but he felt that continuing at his present work was not satisfactory. He talked with Rev. Potts and on his advice decided to become a minister.

Lovejoy acted quickly. Within two weeks after he had made his decision he sold his share of the St. Louis *Times*.

The February 18, 1832, edition contained his farewell message to his readers. He explained that "circumstances most unexpected" and "of a personal character" had forced him to withdraw from the paper. He enjoyed his work as editor even though he found the job a hard one. He was leaving the position with no hard feelings toward anyone, "whether friend or foe." He included a religious message in which he pointed out that without "the religion of the Bible neither civil nor intellectual freedom can long exist."

The next week the new editors explained: "The former editor retired from his office from causes and reasons which had nothing to do with the concerns of the paper."

Lovejoy soon was heading for Princeton Theological Seminary in Princeton, N. J., where most of the Presbyterian ministers were being trained. He did not know that he was making his last trip to the East.

4

BACK TO THE FRONTIER

In March of 1832 Lovejoy enrolled at Princeton's seminary. He was then 29.

When summer arrived, he returned to Maine for his last visit in that area. One of the reasons he returned for a Maine visit rather than continue his studies through the summer was that his father was having "fits of morbid melancholy." His father had always been easily depressed, and this condition was getting worse. In one letter Lovejoy refers to his father as having "a mind diseased." By this time three of the nine Lovejoy children had died, and this weighed heavily on his father's mind. Particularly touching to him was the death of Daniel — the son named after him — who died after some heavy drinking. It was more than the sad-natured father could bear, and his mind cracked temporarily under the strain. When Elijah came home for his summer visit, he found his mother holding up well under all the strain, and he wrote, "I have never seen her equal."

While visiting in Maine he did a little preaching in area churches, but soon headed back for Princeton.

As brilliant a student at the seminary as he had been in college, he completed his seminary training in 13 months, a course that usually took about 3 years.

He was licensed to do his practice preaching in the Philadelphia area. From there he went to Newport, R. I., for several weeks and then to New York City for a few months. He thought about returning to Maine to be near his parents, but all these places had only limited appeal. As a pastor he could have had a comfortable life and work in the East. This was particularly true since word had spread among the ministers of his high scholastic standing and he was regarded as a minister with a bright future. But the area that really needed to have Christianity preached to it was the West.

In August his father died. A man of limited means and abilities, he had lived long enough to see his son prepare for the ministry. By the time Elijah learned of his father's death he had already been buried. Elijah was planning to make a trip from New York to Maine to spend some time with his mother when he received an important message from St. Louis.

A group of Christian businessmen had resolved to start a newspaper in St. Louis that would promote "religion, morality, and education." They were looking for an editor who knew how to run a newspaper and who either was a minister or had some prestige among the ministry. They felt that such a man could do much to change the sinful ways of the frontier town of St. Louis.

The man who had this combination of talents was Elijah Lovejoy, and it took no time to convince him to return to the frontier.

A young man named Andrew Benton had actually tried to get the religious paper under way two years earlier, had issued some announcements about it, and stirred up some interest. Benton did not have the right combination of talents and money to get it going, however, and the task fell to Lovejoy. Several area businessmen said they would back the project financially.

Lovejoy wrote his brother: "They are impatiently calling me to the West, and to the West I must go."

Before he left New York, he was commissioned by the American Home Missionary Society to do preaching for them also. He planned to combine this evangelistic work with his editing.

He felt the needs in St. Louis were so pressing that he decided to return there immediately rather than go to Maine to visit his mother.

He arrived in St. Louis on November 12, 1833 — three days after his 31st birthday. Four years later a mound of fresh earth would mark his grave.

5

EDITOR, PREACHER, AND FIGHTER

Lovejoy was not a man to let any "grass grow under his feet." Ten days after he arrived in St. Louis the first issue of the St. Louis *Observer* appeared. On the masthead were the words: "Jesus Christ, and Him Crucified." The contents clearly showed that this was basically a religious newspaper. A typical issue carried articles on "Original Sin," "The Missionary Enterprise," "A Revival Scene," "Report of the Fourth Annual Meeting of the Illinois Sunday School Union," and smaller news items about religious activity in the nation.

A Philadelphia newspaper noted that it was "as well printed as any of our Eastern periodicals."

There were a few advertisements — very few compared with the other St. Louis newspapers. Since advertising is a newspaper's main source of income, the early issues clearly indicated that Lovejoy would eventually run into financial trouble.

There were occasional references to slavery, but the first enemies of the editor of the *Observer* were made not by his slavery articles but by his religious presentations.

In the 1830s men had strong opinions, if any at all, particularly in matters of faith. Rumors and emotion combined to make men do and say strange things in the guise of religion. Lovejoy was intolerant of those who did not share his Presbyterian beliefs — and there were not many Presbyterians in St. Louis. He was particularly intolerant of Roman Catholics. It was not simply a matter of disagreeing on certain doctrines; he condemned anyone associated with the Roman Catholic Church. It was characteristic of the age he lived in to express extreme opinions, and his were extreme.

While the Roman Catholics were his number-one target, he took out after other groups also, including Baptists and "Campbellites" (Disciples of Christ). His articles attacking one religious group after another assure us that like all other heroes he was a human being and made mistakes.

Inevitably Lovejoy soon collected a sizable group of enemies — people who did not appreciate his strong Presbyterian lectures. What part this may have played in the final drama is hard to know. Undoubtedly Lovejoy could have made and kept friends by stating his views more tactfully. At the very least he silenced some people who otherwise might have come to his defense.

However, his writing was not confined to religious matters. Although slavery was rarely mentioned for some time in his paper, other items and comments appeared:

DESERVED PUNISHMENT

A fellow has been lately sentenced to an imprisonment of four months at New Haven, for having insulted females on the street.

The drawing of lotteries and sale of lottery tickets ceased in New York on the 26th of December. When will they cease here?

On Monday last a woman without arms was married at Bury, the ring being placed by the bridegroom upon one of the bride's toes.

It is difficult for persons living in the older countries to realize the rapidity with which towns and villages spring into existence in the West. Chicago is situated near the northeastern extremity of Illinois. Last spring there were in Chicago five or six stores, now there are from 20 to 25; then there were 150 inhabitants, now from 800 to 1,000.

TOBACCO

A young man of our acquaintance has foolishly addicted himself to the practice of chewing this filthy weed.

Public executions are injurious to the morals of a community.

JACKSONVILLE COLLEGE

We had the pleasure of attending the late Commencement at this Institution. There were no graduates, as the college has not been in operation long enough.

These excerpts provide a bit of the flavor of the newspaper he published. Some items were strange, some humorous, but most fell into neither category — they were lengthy articles about technical theological subjects that could not have interested many people in the frontier city of St. Louis.

There were some practical difficulties running a newspaper with little advertising. After 11 months in business he wrote: "There are now due to us from subscribers several hundred dollars, for the want of which we are most seriously embarrassed. By their conduct they are endangering the very existence of the *Observer*." A month later he pleaded his case again: "The *Observer* is today a year old. The paper — and it need not be disguised — is in a very precarious condition. It is in debt, and is getting into debt every week. Now this state of things cannot continue much longer." Another issue indicated he was receiving no salary.

The Illinois Presbyterian Synod voted to encourage subscribers to the *Observer* because of the "importance of a religious periodical" and in view of the financial "embarrassments of the establishment."

Lovejoy's appeals met with some success, for the paper continued, and a month later there was an advertisement: "WANTED — An apprentice to the printing business, one who can come well recommended, from 12 to 15 years of age." Earlier in the year an advertisement appeared three times: "Wanted to hire, a healthy negro woman, acquainted with all kinds of house work. Enquire at this office."

Illness plagued Lovejoy, and for several issues he was unable to serve as editor. He then returned, "though still with trembling hand." Another time he wrote: "We have put the above article together with the fever rioting in our veins, the headache holding high jubilee in our temples."

In the midst of all his business difficulties Lovejoy was starting to take a stand on the issue of slavery. It was done quietly at first, usually quoting a comment from some other newspaper or magazine.

What prompted his first strong stand was a statement in the newspaper he formerly owned, the St. Louis *Times,* which called for mob action against some women who had started a Sunday school for slaves. While Lovejoy made it clear that he was not an abolitionist (in favor of immediate freedom for slaves), he sided squarely with the women who were teaching the slaves. "Bind their bodies in whatever chains you please," he wrote, "they have souls as precious as those of their masters." The idea that slaves should not be taught religion, as the *Times* suggested, he found "monstrous" and "horrible." That paper's attitude was "shameful" and "savage," he said. As to teaching religion, his answer was simple: "God commands it."

In an editorial he finally decided that "slavery as it now exists among us, must cease to exist."

Two touching articles — probably involving the same man — appeared. Lovejoy quoted in part from the *Missouri Republican,* also published in St. Louis. A man "purchased a negro woman, under the following circumstances. She was about 24 years old, of excellent character, and married to a husband about 28 years of age. As soon as the bargain was closed the driver told her to start, giving her only ten minutes to prepare. She was not allowed to see her husband. She, however, sent him word that she was gone, and bade him good-bye. . . . When the poor fellow, her husband, heard the message he seemed absolutely stunned with the most unexpected blow. He followed his poor wife to town to take a last look, but the thought of parting was more than he could bear." He tried to escape. When they caught him, they "first flogged him severely, but finding the wretched man not sufficiently sensitive, they took him out into the woods and, laying him across some rails, they inflicted the blows with a saw on his bare back and shoulders. The poor man was then corded to a board for the night, and the next day chained." Lovejoy noted that though this man's "face is not as white, his blood is as red and as warm as your own."

After a year it was not uncommon to read in Lovejoy's paper about "the groans of the wretched," "lacerated bodies of helpless men, and women, and children," and "weeping mothers torn from helpless babes."

He soon noted in an editorial — printed in italics so it would stand out — that there is "a great and a very criminal apathy of feeling among the Christians of Missouri, as it respects the condition of our slaves."

But in all of this he made clear that he was not an abolitionist. He favored a gradual solution to the problem. He called those who were seeking immediate freedom for the slaves "unwise, inconsiderate, and headstrong."

When he discovered that his brother Joseph in Maine was an abolitionist, he wrote to him: "I regret, deeply regret, that you cannot see the true effect of all such measures." He told his brother that those who ask for immediate freedom for slaves "are riveting the very chains you seek to break." As to the leader of the abolitionists, Lovejoy asked his brother: "How can you hold communion with such a foul-mouthed fellow?" When a group of women in the East announced that they were starting a paper urging freeing of the slaves, he editorially called their action "unwise." Another time he said that abolitionists are "devoid alike of pity, of humanity, and of shame."

But as objective as he felt he was, he nevertheless was living in a slave state. Many people wanted no one to indicate that even gradual freedom for slaves was a good thing. His occasional references to slavery being a bad thing were upsetting people; he was getting mail asking why he did not "let a certain subject alone." Lovejoy responded: "We do let it alone whenever it is possible so to do. But sometimes it is not possible."

Actually, by comparison with other subjects, slavery was not frequently mentioned during the first year and a half of his work. He was spending much more time in denouncing "Popery" and "Sabbath-trampling, mission-hating Baptists."

When a mob destroyed a combination tavern, gambling house, and house of prostitution, he sounded a warning that would soon be significant: "In this particular case of Monday night, the end accomplished was a good one — a den of drunkenness and impurity was broken up, a public nuisance was abated. But this was done in an illegal manner; and it surely is a most incongruous method of vindicating the laws, by trampling on them ourselves. . . . Who is secure in life or property if the laws are placed at the mercy of a phrensied rabble?"

Almost every issue carried warnings of the dangers of drinking — and the same issues carried the wholesale prices on wine in St. Louis.

Tobacco also continued to be an object of attack. In one issue he announced a "declaration of war against this filthy, poisonous, nauseating, noxious, foul, pestiferous weed."

In addition to his editorial duties he was doing some preaching and some work with religious societies that took him around the state.

On one of these trips he met a beautiful girl from St. Charles, Mo., Celia Ann French. On March 4, 1835, they were married in St. Charles by Rev. William S. Potts, the Presbyterian pastor who had persuaded Lovejoy to enter the ministry.

Lovejoy wrote to his mother that his wife was "tall, well-shaped, of a light, fair complexion . . . large blue eyes . . . In short, she is very beautiful. . . . I need not tell you that she is pious. . . . She is, I know, intelligent, refined, and of agreeable manners; and unless I have entirely mistaken her character, she is also sweet-tempered, obliging, kind-hearted, industrious, good-humoured, and possessed alike of a sound judgment and correct taste. . . . In addition to all this, she loves me."

She was 21; he was 32.

Their married life was exciting — and short. In less than three years she was a widow.

6

DANGER BECOMES A PART OF LIFE

A few months prior to being married Lovejoy attended a meeting of the Presbyterian Synod of Missouri and was among the minority who took an open stand against slavery.

More and more he was publicly supporting freedom for the slaves.

He had been ordained as an evangelist by the Presbyterians of the St. Louis area; when he went about the area preaching, although slavery was not the main topic of his sermons, slavery was part of them.

His newspaper was talking in plainer language with almost every issue. When the editor of a New Orleans religious newspaper announced he would permit no more discussion of slavery in his paper, Lovejoy wrote in an editorial: "If the Christians of Louisiana and Mississippi cannot bear the discussion of this subject, they may as well give up their religious newspaper altogether."

Yet he still said he was not for immediate freedom for all slaves. He wanted them to be freed gradually, and he was opposed to slaves running away from their masters.

But the talk in the streets made no fine distinctions between those who were for gradual freedom and those who were for immediate freedom. Because Lovejoy was for freeing the slaves, this made him an abolitionist in the eyes of most people, and in their eyes this was not good.

One of the top officers in the First Presbyterian Church in St. Louis frequently visited Lovejoy during the summer following his marriage and urged him to stop writing about slavery. He said that Lovejoy was in real danger of action by a mob.

Others were telling him the same, but Lovejoy paid no attention.

In September Lovejoy went to a religious "camp meeting" near Potosi, Mo., a town about 60 miles from St. Louis. Word had spread ahead of Lovejoy about his views on slavery. What he said stirred up things even more.

His return schedule to St. Louis called for passing through the town of Potosi during the afternoon. When this became known, two men decided that they would waylay Lovejoy in order to tar and feather him. The plan was to do literally just that: cover his body with hot tar, put chicken feathers on the tar, and then display him.

Lovejoy knew nothing about the plot, but at the last minute he changed his plans and did not leave until the next morning. The two men, tired of waiting, gave up the idea. Lovejoy learned about their plan on his way to St. Louis.

When he got into St. Louis, he discovered that a handbill had been circulated, urging mob action to tear down the *Observer*. "*The Missouri Argus* openly called upon the hurrah boys to mob me down," Lovejoy wrote his brother Joseph.

If Lovejoy was frightened, it did not show in his newspaper. It continued on the same course.

To add to the tenseness of the situation, Lovejoy, in his capacity as a representative of a Bible Society, sent some Bibles to Jefferson City, Mo. He needed some papers to stuff around the Bibles; apparently without giving it a second thought, he used some old antislavery newspapers for the purpose. When the box containing the Bibles was opened in Jefferson City, the antislavery papers caused an uproar. A friend immediately wrote urging him to "act with caution." The situation was so tense, said this friend, that when the antislavery literature was discovered, someone could have "blown up a blast with but little encouragement." The *Commercial Bulletin* was a new newspaper in St. Louis; its editor commented on this incident, viewing it as a terrible thing. No man should send antislavery literature "in the same parcel with the sacred volume! Is this his religion? Is this his 'good will to all men'?" The editorial added ominously that Lovejoy was being "watched," that his "slightest movement" would bring punishment, and that he would be "put down." Lovejoy called the editor "well-meaning but weak-minded." Lovejoy was told that if he had been in Jefferson City when the Bibles arrived, he would undoubtedly have been the victim of a mob.

Lovejoy responded in his newspaper:

> I am not aware that any law of my country forbids my sending what document I please to a friend or citizen. I know, indeed, that *mob-law* has decided otherwise. . . . I have never knowingly sent any abolition publication to a single individual in Missouri or elsewhere; I claim the *right* to send ten thousand of them if I choose. Whether I will *exercise* that right or not, is for me, and not for the *mob,* to decide.

He then quoted the state constitution: "Every person may freely speak, write, and print *on any subject."*

He added: "The truth is, my fellow citizens, if you give ground a single inch, there is no stopping place. I deem it, therefore, my duty to take my stand upon the Constitution."

To add to the tenseness in the St. Louis area, five slaves escaped into Illinois about this same time. A posse of 60 men was formed to get them. The posse crossed into neighboring Illinois, where it was assumed the slaves had fled. Illinois was a free state with some strong Southern ties and sympathies, and there was no objection to Missouri residents crossing the border to recover their "property" that had escaped.

Escaping slaves were not too difficult to find. They were dark-skinned among a population of mostly white-skinned people. In addition, their "Negro clothes" — clothing ordinarily worn by slaves — distinguished them from any free Negroes in Illinois.

It was not long before the posse of 60 men found the slaves, and found two white men who, someone charged, had helped the slaves escape. The slaves and the two white men were taken back to St. Louis.

A hanging structure was quickly fixed in a wooded spot near St. Louis, and at first the two white men were threatened with immediate death. There was some hesitancy, however, because neither man confessed to any guilt and because some Methodists in the group assembled did not believe in execution.

Someone shouted that they should be whipped first, then after they had confessed, should be hanged. There was division in the group again on this, whether there should be an immediate hanging or the whipping first. Finally they decided on the whipping.

Each of the approximately 60 men present was to give each of the two white men five lashes with the whip. They were told they would be whipped until they confessed. After one victim had received about 150 lashes, he cried out that he was guilty. The other man was given another 50 lashes and still professed that he was innocent. It was clear the second man would die before he would admit guilt. The two were then locked in jail.

No evidence was ever produced that either was guilty, and they were eventually released.

But this incident — plus riots and mob scenes around the country — had people stirred up, and in St. Louis Lovejoy was the center of the tension.

At the end of September Lovejoy left to go to Union, Mo., for an area Presbyterian meeting, followed by a statewide meeting at Marion, Mo. At Union he introduced some antislavery resolutions which were adopted unanimously. At Marion he ran into difficulty, for a church official coming directly from St. Louis reported "a thousand frightful things" about the happenings in St. Louis. People were exceedingly angry, and mob action was almost inevitable, he told them. Other reports from St. Louis were similar.

The result was that the antislavery resolutions did not pass, and there was fear for Lovejoy's life. He was advised not to go back to St. Louis.

His wife was in St. Charles, Mo., where he had taken her for safety, particularly because she was expecting their first child and was not in good health.

"The brethren told me I had no right to sacrifice her, whatever I might do with myself," Lovejoy wrote his brother. When he got to St. Charles, he found his wife still sick, and for three days Lovejoy, too, was ill. "By this time I had fully made up my mind that duty to my Lord and Master required my presence at St. Louis. My friends advised me not to go; *all but my wife*. She said, *'Go if you think duty calls you.'* Accordingly I came into St. Louis." He left his wife temporarily in St. Charles.

While he was away from St. Louis, a number of things had happened. People had become even more excited, and tension was in the air.

The first issue of the *Observer* that appeared while he was absent at the Presbyterian synod had this notice:

Since the Editor left, the Publishers of the *Observer* have received a communication from the owners of this paper, advising an entire suspension of all controversy upon the exciting subject of slavery. As this course is entirely agreeable to the feelings and views of the publishers, nothing upon

the subject will appear in its columns during the absence of
the Editor. Upon his return the communication will be sub-
mitted to him, and the future course of the paper finally
arranged.

Those who had attended the meeting of owners included
many of his friends. Some were frightened for Lovejoy, some
for themselves. The greatest disappointment to Lovejoy was
that one of those at this meeting was the minister of the First
Presbyterian Church, Rev. William Potts, the man who had
persuaded Lovejoy to enter the ministry and the man who
had married him.

When Lovejoy refused to change his position, the owners
demanded that he resign as editor. Lovejoy had no choice.
He thought he had lost the fight. The owners then turned
the property over to the man who held the mortgage. That
man had no use for printing equipment without an editor,
and he surprised everyone, including Lovejoy, by asking the
controversial editor to stay on.

While Lovejoy was gone, there had been more and more
talk about mob action against him. One group actually formed
a mob and was going to attack the *Observer* office, but when
the owners threatened gunfire for anyone attacking the plant,
they changed their minds. One of the local newspapers, in
commenting on Lovejoy, noted ominously that the church
would soon be free of "the rotten sheep in it."

If people expected all this to frighten Lovejoy away from
his stand, they were badly mistaken. He stood firm — even
stronger than before. This was despite the fact that he was
now a father as well as a husband. In March — one year after
his marriage — Celia Ann gave birth to a son.

When the slavery supporters saw Lovejoy's firm stand, it
made them even more furious. A meeting of citizens passed
a resolution to stop all antislavery talk and specifically Lovejoy and his newspaper. Resolutions of the meeting called

Lovejoy and his friends "misguided fanatics." The meeting
also pointed out that freedom of speech does not give the right
"to freely discuss the question of slavery, either orally or
through the medium of the press." Slavery, the resolutions
said, was "too nearly allied to the vital interests of the slaveholding States" to be publicly discussed. The meeting called
for the appointment of a "Committee of Vigilance" to see that
their wishes were carried out in case city officials failed to act.
The Committee of Vigilance was composed of 7 persons from
each ward, 20 for the St. Louis suburbs, and 7 for each township in St. Louis County.

It was clearly a call for mob action!

Lovejoy responded with fighting words, admitting that he
was writing and publishing them at the peril of his life. He
would give in neither to the owners who wanted to muzzle
him nor to the mob who wanted to silence him. He wrote:
"I am threatened with violence and death because I dare to
advocate, in any way, the cause of the oppressed. Under a deep
sense of my obligations to my country, the church and my
God, I declare it to be my fixed purpose to submit to no such
dictation. *And I am prepared to abide the consequences.*"

He added words which he would repeat in Alton soon —
words for which he would be remembered more than any
others: "I can die at my post, but I cannot desert it."

He urged mob leaders not to damage the *Observer* office.
He said that the office belongs "to the young men who print
the paper; and they are in no way responsible for the matter
appearing in its columns. If the popular vengeance needs
a victim, I offer myself a willing sacrifice."

Lovejoy said he faced death with no misgiving, but for "one
string tugging at my heart": the concern for his wife. He said
he faced death "freely forgiving my enemies, even those who
thirst for my blood."

But his editorials did not express a mere passive willingness to accept the consequences of what he had written. He vigorously restated his earlier stands and went beyond them.

He repeated that he could not see how the Bible could approve tearing families apart "and then driving them with a whip, like so many mules, to a distant market, there to be disposed of to the highest bidder."

Lovejoy went on to attack the most sensitive problem of all. His accusers had called him an "amalgamationist," a term used to describe those who believed in the intermarriage of the two races. Lovejoy denied that he favored interracial marriage; but he hinted publicly at what was never printed — that sexual abuse of Negro women by white slaveowners was common. The worst treatment of the Negro is not the public whipping, he wrote, but what takes place "in their cabins." Everyone knew what he meant. He was not an "amalgamationist," but he noted that there are some "practical amalgamationists." Then he added: "Unless my eyes deceive me as I walk the streets of our city, there are some among us who venture to put it into practice."

No one had ever talked like that in print in St. Louis.

Lovejoy took off a few days from St. Louis to conduct some religious services. When he returned he was told: "It will no longer be safe for you to be on the streets of St. Louis — either by day or night."

7

A HORRIBLE MURDER

Lovejoy lived from day to day never knowing whether he would ever see another sunset.

The tension of the fall of 1835 carried over into December, when a handbill was printed for another mass meeting to "put down the vile slander of E. P. Lovejoy." The meeting was held. Once again those present demanded that Lovejoy "discontinue any further publications in that paper on the subject of slavery."

Another St. Louis newspaper now entered the picture forcefully. The *Missouri Republican* said that meetings like the one just described "are productive of much more harm than good." The *Missouri Republican* called on citizens *not* to unite "in a crusade against the liberty of the press."

This was the first time so powerful a force had stood up squarely — not in agreement with Lovejoy, but in defense of his right to express whatever opinions he had. That, plus the cooling effects of winter, calmed things down somewhat for a short while.

Just prior to that time Lovejoy made a trip to Alton, considering a move to the free territory of Illinois at the suggestion of the new owner. Alton area civic and religious leaders were enthusiastic about the idea. But Lovejoy decided to stay in St. Louis. He felt that some might regard his moving away as a flight from danger. Besides, the worst period of tension appeared to be past. He still was keeping Alton in the back of his mind, however, because a few months later he had a few lines about what a fine place Alton is and of the "spirit of liberality" there which he had heard about.

On top of his other troubles Lovejoy was still having financial problems. The Illinois Synod of the Presbyterian Church had heard about Lovejoy's strong antislavery stand and by resolution withdrew its support of the *Observer*. Six ministers at the meeting strongly protested such action, and perhaps as a compromise the Synod passed an antislavery resolution. But the withdrawal of support of the *Observer* stood. Lovejoy editorially said he was having financial troubles and that subscribers would have to pay their subscriptions if the *Observer* was to continue to "dare to speak out freely." In a letter he said the *Observer* could continue only "if the Christian public will support it."

But Lovejoy also received encouragement. Rev. Edward Beecher, president of the new college at Jacksonville, Ill. (and brother of the future author of *Uncle Tom's Cabin*), wrote, enclosing $20 and stating that between $100 and $200 more would be raised for the paper. Beecher said Lovejoy had spoken "with the courage demanded in a soldier of the cross." He also wrote: "The time for silence has gone by."

In a letter to his mother in Maine, Lovejoy showed a little more confidence in his situation: "Finding that I am not to be driven nor frightened away, they are beginning to feel and act a little more reasonably." He also wrote about a slaveowner in St. Louis who whipped his female slave to death. "Such men are not molested; but he who ventures to say that slavery is a sin, does it at the risk of his life."

On New Year's Eve of 1835 his newspaper noted "the baptism of an infant slave. It was the first case of the kind we ever witnessed."

There continued to be letters to the newspaper and editorial comments on slavery, including the blunt declaration "Slavery is a *sin.*" But life was gradually becoming a little more peaceful. This did not mean that people in St. Louis liked him or what he said. There merely did not seem to be much they could do about it.

Suddenly the issue exploded!

It was caused by the murder of one man and the burning alive of another.

Witnesses and newspaper accounts differ somewhat on minor details, but here is the sad, gruesome story:

Francis McIntosh was a free Negro who worked as a porter and cook on the steamboat *Flora,* which was docked in St. Louis on Thursday afternoon, April 28, 1836. Also docked there was the *Lady Jackson.* Both boats had been in Louisville. McIntosh had met a free Negro girl from the *Lady Jackson* in Louisville and had fallen in love with her. A crew member of the *Flora* described McIntosh as a "quiet, good-natured Negro." The girl he fell in love with was the chambermaid aboard the *Lady Jackson.* The *Lady Jackson* got to St. Louis a few hours ahead of the boat on which McIntosh was working. When the *Flora* arrived and McIntosh was through with his work, he put on a bright-red jacket which had been given him by a New Orleans gambler and walked off the boat, intending to visit the girl on the *Lady Jackson.*

Exactly what happened next is not clear. The captain of the *Flora* said that two officers — not in uniform — were chasing a man and shouted at McIntosh to stop the pursued man when he went past. Whether for fear or because he did not know they were officers, McIntosh did nothing and was arrested.

The other version of the arrest is that two other members of the *Flora* crew had been drinking and were getting into trouble with the officers. McIntosh tried to help them and was arrested.

Regardless of which story is true, McIntosh was arrested by George Hammond, deputy sheriff, and William Mull, deputy constable. McIntosh was taken before the justice of the peace and charged with "breach of the peace." He was ordered to jail. For a free Negro to be arrested in a slave state was a frightening prospect. It might mean a return to slavery. He asked Hammond and Mull how long he would have to be in jail. What they told him is again not clear. There is a conflict in testimony. But he apparently was told that he would be in jail from five years to life. He had no attorney, and he knew that as a Negro he would get none in Missouri.

McIntosh suddenly turned on the two men who had him under arrest, pulled a knife, and lunged first at Mull. He missed him, but quickly lunged again, caught Mull on the right side of his chest, and wounded him seriously. Crazed with fear, he then turned on Hammond, who was holding his shoulder, struck the lower part of Hammond's chin and neck, cutting the jugular vein. Hammond started to flee, walked about 60 feet, and dropped dead, bleeding profusely.

A small crowd had gathered to watch the Negro being taken to jail but was stunned into inaction during the deadly fight which had taken only seconds. When Hammond had been wounded, McIntosh started to run. Mull, despite his serious wound, and some others followed McIntosh, shouting for his capture. McIntosh was quickly caught and placed in jail.

In the meantime Hammond's widow was told about her husband's death, and she and her children came and found him dead on the street in a pool of blood, surrounded by a group of curious and sympathetic townspeople. Mrs. Hammond had some type of obvious physical handicap — what, we do not know. The scene of this physically handicapped woman, suddenly a widow, and her children screaming and crying beside the body of Hammond, was moving. Hammond was well liked; Lovejoy described him as "an intelligent, upright man, and an excellent officer." The scene was so moving, in fact, that those gathered there had a strong desire to see justice done immediately, to "get the nigger that done this."

McIntosh offered virtually no further resistance when he was caught. Reports differ greatly about his capture. He was a terribly frightened Negro who knew he had committed a serious crime against a white man.

It seemed only minutes after the slaying took place that crowds started collecting, and the demand grew for immediate vengeance. Soon the crowd had become a mob, moved to the jail, and asked for McIntosh.

The sheriff at first tried to resist the crowd, but his family occupied a part of the jail as living quarters, and he feared for their safety. Rather than turn McIntosh over to the mob — which he knew would violate his sworn duty — he took his family and escaped, leaving McIntosh locked in the jail but taking the keys with him.

The mob continued to demand McIntosh's life, and the absence of the sheriff increased their determination.

One man — not identified in any newspaper — stood up and tried to halt them. He said that the courts would handle the matter quickly. But that was not quick enough for the growing mob, and the man saw that he would lose his life if he continued his opposition.

Soon tools were brought to break down the door. While men worked at getting the doors down, an intense quiet settled over the crowd. Those who spoke did it in whispers. Others were armed and stood by to make sure no one would stop them in their course.

It took more than an hour to get through the jail doors to McIntosh's cell. When the prisoner was reached there was a shout of triumph from this crowd that wanted blood. McIntosh was dragged out of the jail and then seized by the crowd. Some grabbed him by the legs, some the arms, and one grabbed his hair. In this way he was marched to the edge of town — not far from the jail — by a crowd now numbering several thousand.

McIntosh was then chained to a large locust tree, his back against the trunk of the tree, facing the South and facing the people who brought him there. Wood, consisting mainly of rail ties and old planks, was piled around him as high as his knees. Shavings were brought and a hot brand was obtained — the kind used to brand horses and livestock. The brand was touched to the shavings and a fire started.

Up to this point McIntosh had said nothing. When the fire started, he begged for someone in the crowd to shoot him. No one moved to offer him help. One report has it that a lawyer named Riddle wanted the crowd to see what a terrible thing they had done, and for that reason helped to prevent people from shooting him. This story seems doubtful. The other accounts contain no such incident.

In any event, when McIntosh screamed for someone to shoot him, no one did. From that point on he sang hymns and prayed while the crowd watched. After a few minutes his features became disfigured by the flames, and he was silent. Someone said that he apparently was out of his misery, and McIntosh replied distinctly: "No, no. I feel as much as any of you. I hear you all. Shoot me! Shoot me!" Between 10 and 20 minutes after the fire was started McIntosh was dead.

An old Negro named Louis was given 75 cents for keeping the fire burning during the night.

The crowd apparently was quiet and orderly after the death

and disappeared quickly, a few to taverns but most to their homes.

The next morning a black and disfigured corpse was all that remained. A group of boys started throwing stones at the remains, the object of their game to see who could first succeed in breaking the skull.

Lovejoy was deeply moved and depressed by all this. In the next issue of the *Observer* he wrote, "We visited the scene of the burning on the day following, about noon. We stood and gazed for a moment or two, upon the blackened and mutilated trunk — for that was all which remained — of McIntosh before us, and as we turned away, in bitterness of heart we prayed that we might not live."

A week later he was still so moved by what had happened that he continued to pray for death.

Lovejoy was intense in his attack on what happened. While he talked plainer than did the other newspaper, the *Missouri Republican* also found the mob action "revolting." Across the Mississippi River the newly established Alton *Telegraph* likewise condemned the mob action. In Springfield, Ill., a young state legislator named Abraham Lincoln gave a talk before the Young Men's Lyceum, warning against "the growing disposition to substitute the wild and furious passions" for the law. Lincoln talked about "worse than savage mobs" at "that horror-striking scene in St. Louis."

Lovejoy spared no words in condemning the mob. He described the whispering at the scene as whispers "which made the blood curdle to hear." He said the whole thing was "savage barbarity." He called upon all who participated — which must have been the majority of the population — to "seek forgiveness." No one could have spoken stronger or with more courage against the "spirit of mobism." Lovejoy wrote: "In Charlestown it burns a Convent over the head of defenseless women . . . in Vicksburg it hangs up gamblers, three or four in a row; and in St. Louis it forces a man . . . to the stake and burns him alive!"

The next week the *Missouri Republican* noted that some Eastern abolitionists were trying to gather together the bones of McIntosh "with the intention of forwarding them to the Atlantic States. The use to be made of them there, must be obvious." The *Missouri Republican* warned the people of the Eastern states to be "upon their guard" for this "dastardly means" of promoting the antislavery cause.

The strong Lovejoy stand in the *Observer* was greeted unfavorably by the public. There were not only threats of violence again, but also some actual minor damage done to the *Observer* office. One night the composing sticks were stolen, a piece of equipment vital in 1836 to produce a newspaper when there was no automatic typesetting equipment. The next noon — when everyone was out to lunch — more equipment was stolen. A week later the completed form for printing the newspaper was destroyed.

The *Observer* commented: "Any information which may lead to the detection of those engaged in this *mean business* will be gratefully received."

These things happened while Lovejoy and his wife were in Pittsburgh, attending the national meeting of the Presbyterian Church. He was the official delegate for the Presbyterians in the St. Louis area. While in Pittsburgh he was part of a sizable minority that was defeated 154—87 in an attempt to get the Presbyterian Church nationally to take a strong stand against slavery. The motion that prevailed was to postpone indefinitely any action on the issue. Lovejoy and 26 others then filed a protest which was entered into the proceedings.

When the convention was over, he and his wife headed back to St. Louis. They stopped four days in Peoria and confided to some friends that they were thinking of moving their operation to Alton.

When they returned, Lovejoy noted in an editorial comment: "After an absence lengthened considerably beyond his expectations, the Editor has returned to his duties. He comes back with health even better than when he left, and, as he trusts, with renewed purpose to spend and be spent in the service of his Divine Master."

Before the Lovejoys arrived in St. Louis they heard about the damage which had been done to the *Observer* equipment. The account of the conduct of the judge who was handling the investigation of the mob slaying of the free Negro amazed them.

The man before whom the mob action against McIntosh was taken was Judge Luke Edward Lawless, a man of controversy in the community, who had himself once served time in jail for contempt of court. Judge Lawless was 53 years old and satisfied with the community's culture — slavery and all. His name fits the story as if it were fiction.

When the matter came before his court, Judge Lawless told the grand jury that what happened to the Negro, Francis McIntosh, was contrary to law and was a tragedy.

From there Judge Lawless proceeded to make one of the most amazing speeches to the grand jury in the history of our country's courts. First, he practically told the grand jury not to find anyone guilty of the McIntosh slaying, and then he proceeded to blame Lovejoy for what happened!

Judge Lawless told the grand jury: "If the destruction of the murderer of Hammond was the act of congregated thousands, seized by an almost electric frenzy, which, in all ages and nations, has hurried on the infuriated multitude to deeds of death and destruction, then, I say, act not at all in the matter; the case is beyond the reach of human law."

In the course of his remarks to the grand jury, Judge Lawless said that he had saved Lovejoy and the *Observer* office

from destruction because of Lovejoy's remarks over the Mc-
Intosh slaying. ("We do not believe him," Lovejoy wrote.)

True or not — it may have been true — Judge Lawless then
went on to condemn Lovejoy and the *Observer* instead of the
mob and its leaders.

Newspapers like the *Observer* "fanaticize the negro and ex-
cite him against the white man," Judge Lawless told the grand
jury. The judge then cited several quotations from the *Observer,* including the following sentence: "Slavery is a sin and
ought to be abandoned." The judge told the jurors: "It seems
to me impossible, that while such language is used and published as that which I have cited from the St. Louis *Observer,*
there can be safety in a slaveholding state."

The judge also noted the last sentence of a letter to the
editor which read: "Heaven grant I may never be the master
of a slave." Judge Lawless said that this type of language
urged Negroes to revolt.

Then Judge Lawless asked for action against Lovejoy.

"It is all important," he said, "that the negro population
within our bounds should be saved from the corrupting influence to which I have thought it my duty to call your attention. . . . But it will be asked, is there no remedy for this
monstrous evil? I am compelled to answer that I know of none.
No law exists, that I know of, to punish this crime against the
peace and rights of the people of Missouri." He asked the
grand jury to consider what could be done. The judge said
he was for freedom of the press, but he could "see no reason
why the Press should be a means of widespread mischief. . . .
Are we to be the victims of those sanctimonious madmen?"

He added that he hoped the next session of the legislature
would adopt measures "to punish, if they cannot prevent,
those exhortations to rebellion."

It was an amazing statement for a judge to make — asking
the grand jury not to condemn the leaders of the mob and

asking for action against the man who condemned the illegal mob slaying.

The grand jury did what the judge had told them to do: they found no one guilty.

Reaction to Judge Lawless' speech came rapidly. The New York *American* said it read the speech with "surprise and disgust." It also noted the odd coincidence of his name — Lawless.

The Pittsburgh *Christian Herald* called the judge's statement "an outrage on all law, morality, and decency." The Jacksonville (Ill.) *Patriot* noted that the judge's ideas strike at "the very root of our liberties."

Lovejoy responded as one would expect him to do. He said he would rather "be chained to the same tree as McIntosh and share his fate" than to accept the ideas of Judge Lawless. Lovejoy said that the answer to mobs is to enforce the laws. Until then, mobs will continue to "destroy, plunder and burn."

Lovejoy added: "We covet not the loss of property, nor the honors of martyrdom; but better, far better, that the office of the *Observer* should be scattered in fragments to the four winds than that the doctrines promoted by Judge Lawless from the bench should be adopted in this community." Lovejoy charged that the judge was encouraging future mobs to action.

Between irritating the mob members — which were a majority of the citizens — and various religious groups, Lovejoy had angered almost every powerful group and person in St. Louis.

In writing his editorial Lovejoy not only attacked what the judge said, but, showing one of his weaknesses, he also attacked Judge Lawless because he was a Roman Catholic. A few weeks before that, Lovejoy had made some comments about a Presbyterian minister, Rev. H. Chamberlain, that prompted the minister to put an item in another local paper: "TO THE PUBLIC. The last Saint Louis *Observer* contains an assault on my character, injurious to me as a man, as a citizen of this community, and a minister of the gospel of Christ."

But whatever must be admitted about the bad taste of some of Lovejoy's remarks, there is no excuse for this outrageous advice of a judge. Judge Lawless' statement made clear to the people that the action of a mob would not result in court action against either the mob or its leaders.

One further news item indicated to the potential evildoers that they should act, and act soon. In the same issue that denounced Judge Lawless there was an announcement that Lovejoy would be moving his newspaper operations to Alton.

Because of fear of mob action, particularly to his wife and newborn son, Lovejoy finally decided to move the newspaper to Alton. There he could operate on free territory, he thought, without losing any of his subscribers and influence. It will be recalled that because of constant threats and his wife's poor health, Lovejoy had moved his wife and son to her home in St. Charles. He wanted to face the anger of St. Louis alone. Now, he felt, they could move to Alton, where they could live together without fear of mob action. His announcement stated: "After much deliberation, and consultation with a number of our friends, we have determined hereafter to issue the *Observer* from Alton." He said that he hoped to keep all of his subscribers and that he felt the paper would be "better supported there than it is now."

The conflict in which Lovejoy was involved gave his paper national importance. Subscription lists grew and a few weeks after the McIntosh slaying the *Observer* was able to announce that it would now be "one-third larger." Lovejoy had no intention of losing this growing national influence to a mob.

Perhaps a factor in his decision was that in northern Missouri a mob had driven Rev. David Nelson out of the state. Rev. Nelson was a strong antislavery man and the minister whom Lovejoy credited for his conversion to Christianity. Rev. Nelson made no apologies for his strong antislavery stand, and he spoke with conviction and power. He would not administer the Lord's Supper to anyone who owned slaves. When Rev. Nelson read from the pulpit an appeal for contributions to settle free Negroes in Africa, there was an immediate uproar; a fight broke out and one man was stabbed. All of these things were too much for residents of a slave state, and Rev. Nelson was forced to leave Missouri.

When Lovejoy printed his decision to move to Alton, the Lovejoy haters knew that any action would have to be taken quickly. About 11 o'clock that evening a group of men started roaming the streets of St. Louis. They carried a drum with them and marched from street to street, beating the drum, asking for volunteers to destroy the *Observer's* plant. Because of Judge Lawless' ruling they felt they could act openly and with safety. By midnight they had gathered about 200 men and headed for the *Observer*. In a short time they had broken down the doors and began destroying things and scattering type. Lovejoy's brother John was living with him at the time and had a trunk full of clothing in the office. The mob carried it to the river and threw it in. Much printing equipment was also thrown into the river. Some of it was broken and left in the printshop. In addition, the furniture that Lovejoy and his wife had bought from careful savings was thrown into the river, also some gifts they had received after their marriage. The total damage was "at least $700," according to Lovejoy. In 1836 $700 was a tremendous sum of money.

One of the aldermen of the city, Bryan Mullanphy, tried to stop the mob, but with no success. He had no police backing and could gather no support from any other city officials in time for action. The *Missouri Republican* found the mob action "dreadful" and took a clear stand for law and order: "We put aside altogether the individual whose conduct has

[51]

furnished a pretended excuse for this outrageous violation of the law. His publication may have been imprudent; but that he had a right — a constitutional right — is a position which we hold. . . . Where is this thing to end? . . . Who can feel himself secure when 15 or 20 men are permitted, for hours, to walk through the city, beating up for recruits, and then, without molestation, to break into houses and cast all they contain to the winds? Protect the property of every citizen, no matter how obnoxious he may be to any portion of the community."

Lovejoy's wife — now temporarily in St. Charles — stood up well under all this. He wrote to his mother: "My dear wife is a perfect heroine. Though of delicate health, she endures affliction more calmly than I had supposed possible for a woman to do. Never has she, by a single word, attempted to turn me from the scene of warfare and danger; never has she whispered a feeling of discontent at the hardships to which she had been subjected in consequence of her marriage to me. She has seen me shunned, hated, and reviled, by those who were once my dearest friends. She has heard them curse and threaten me, and she has only clung to me the more closely and more devotedly. When I told her that the mob had destroyed a considerable portion of our furniture, she said: 'It does not matter what they have destroyed since they have not hurt you.' Such is woman! And such is the woman God has given me."

The mayor of the city quickly called for trial of some of the rioters. No one was found guilty.

Many St. Louis friends now urged Lovejoy to stay in St. Louis and fight it out, arguing that to go to Alton would mean giving in to the mob. But Lovejoy decided to go ahead with his plans to move to Alton. His printing press itself was not ruined by the mob, although the large, heavy piece of equipment had been turned over. Lovejoy arranged to send the press to Alton, together with some smaller items of printing equipment that were salvaged.

It will be a thrill to work in territory where there is no slavery, Lovejoy thought.

Little did he imagine that within a few hours after landing in Alton he would again be the victim of a mob.

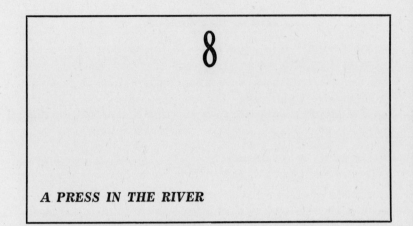

8

A PRESS IN THE RIVER

When Elijah Lovejoy arrived at Alton, he did so with the strong belief that in Illinois there would be more tolerance of antislavery opinions. He had written some articles on political questions for the Alton *Telegraph* — not using his name — and there had been little reaction to his views. However, he knew that the majority of people would not share his opinions — for Illinois had been settled from the south to the north, mostly by Southerners. Illinois almost had become a slave state, and Alton was just across the river from the slave state of Missouri.

When Lovejoy arrived, the official census showed there were 331 slaves in Illinois; slaves, who for one reason or another were exempt from the provisions of the Illinois law and state constitution. In addition, there was "practical slavery" of many more in Illinois. These were Negroes who were technically free but who would "voluntarily" lease or rent themselves to someone for a stated period of years. Not many of the Negroes who signed these documents really knew their contents. It was in a very real sense a limited form of slavery.

Alton was a thriving river town on the Mississippi, and many were confident that Alton would soon pass St. Louis in population. Alton had become the important city of Illinois.

An election in Illinois to determine the capital city ended with Alton as the choice, even though the state legislature did not follow the public's vote in that matter.

Illinois had cities, like Quincy and Jacksonville, where there was strong antislavery sentiment. These areas were giving Lovejoy some support, and he hoped for more now that he was in their state.

A few miles from Alton was the small community of Otterville, where a free Negro was going to a school established there. The Negro's name was George Washington, and he was known in the area as "Black George." He was a respected member of the Otterville community.

Lovejoy's brother John had worked for the Alton *Telegraph,* the new paper in the city, and felt the move to bring the *Observer* to Alton would be a good one.

For these reasons Lovejoy came to Alton in the free state of Illinois with hope. This hope did not last many hours.

The printing press and what other few pieces of printing equipment Lovejoy had salvaged from the wrecking of the plant in St. Louis were shipped on the steamboat *Palmyra.* It landed at the wharf in Alton on a Sunday morning in late July. Lovejoy believed that working on Sunday was sinful. He had requested that the equipment arrive on a day other than Sunday. Since it came on Sunday, he refused to move it, nor did he want to ask Sunday work of the other men who would be needed to move it. But he planned to get men to take the heavy equipment to the new *Observer* office the first thing Monday.

A sad surprise was awaiting him on Monday morning. During Sunday night's darkness some men — reportedly from across the river in Missouri — had knocked the press to pieces and thrown it into the river, together with the other small pieces of equipment he had.

News of this destruction spread quickly throughout Alton,

and a meeting of the leading citizens was called that night. Alton was a law-abiding city, and the general reaction to the destruction of Lovejoy's equipment was one of outrage.

The men who met that night spoke of law and order and the need of protecting the property of all citizens. The mayor was there. The leading businessmen were there, including Winthrop Gilman, a partner of Benjamin Godfrey. Godfrey and Gilman had the largest business in the city, and Godfrey was rumored to be the wealthiest man in the state, a rumor that was probably true.

Gilman, a businessman who was destined to become one of the heroes in the final tragedy, urged that funds be subscribed to get Lovejoy back into the newspaper business, so he might publish a religious newspaper in Alton.

Lovejoy spoke and assured them that he was not an abolitionist — favoring immediate freeing of the slaves — but at the same time said that he was opposed to slavery. He told them that he intended mainly to publish a religious newspaper; he felt that he could devote less space to slavery than he did when he was in St. Louis. "When I was in St. Louis I felt myself called upon to treat at large upon the subject of slavery as I was in a state where the evil existed," he told them. "Now having come to a free state where the evil does not exist, I feel myself less called upon to discuss the subject than when I was in St. Louis."

Then he added these significant words: "But, gentlemen, as long as I am an American citizen, and as long as American blood runs in these veins, I shall hold myself at liberty to speak, to write, and to publish whatever I please on any subject."

What he said impressed them. What remained unsaid was that even in his St. Louis newspaper slavery was not the major topic, except in the few months prior to his quick departure. And much as he would deny being an abolitionist, he would

[56]

nevertheless be regarded as one because he believed slavery wrong and said so. The fine points would not be noticed by people in frontier society, particularly not by men who might get together over some strong homemade whiskey.

The Alton *Telegraph* reported the meeting that night as a "respectable assembly." Those at the meeting "came not to express an opinion upon the subject of Abolition, for on that subject there is no difference of opinion amongst us; but they came to give utterance to the abhorrence felt by all for this infamous outrage upon the private property of an individual. He has the right to form his opinions and the right to express them — and the day the right freely to express our own thoughts is taken from us, that day will be the last of our religious and political freedom."

Lovejoy allowed those at the meeting to receive the impression that he was going to cause no more trouble than any other citizen, that the presence of his *Observer* would not disturb the peace of the city. To that extent he gave them a false view, as they would soon discover.

One of the reasons he gave them this wrong slant was probably because he genuinely felt that he could now leave the issue of slavery somewhat alone. He had no desire to be a "crusader" other than in running a religious newspaper that would bring men closer to God.

By the time the meeting was over in Alton that night Lovejoy had a pledge that he would receive support for his newspaper in Alton. In 12 hours he had seen his hopes for a paper thrown into the river and then revived.

Lovejoy's brother John, who was living with him, was soon less optimistic about Alton than his older brother. He was "completely disgusted with the West." The actions in Saint Louis were "outrageous, uncivilized, fiendish, and dangerous to the preservation of our government." But he found Alton no better. "Tell all the good people in that section of the country who are doing a good business not to leave it and come here. Their property is not safe here; their lives are not safe; and, in fact, nothing is safe. Stay where you are, and live peaceably and happily."

He added: "You may expect some severe articles one of these days. The people here deserve it, and I think they will get it, for you know that Parish* is perfectly able to give them a dose."

As to protection for the press coming from Cincinnati, Lovejoy's brother had a glint in his eyes. His plans were simple. He wrote: "I shall watch it now, and the first person that attempts to come to harm it may expect a small piece of lead to be lodged in him, for it is of no use to trifle with those scoundrels."

But no trouble developed. By September of that year of 1836 Lovejoy had the new printing equipment he needed and had his first issue out. In his first edition from Alton he made clear his stand: "The system of Negro slavery is an awful evil and sin." He also stated clearly that under no circumstances would he give up "the rights of conscience, the freedom of opinion, and of the press."

The first issue talked about the "great enlargement of our paper." The editor noted that the paper needed 2,000 subscribers to make it a thriving business, and at that time there were only 1,000.

One of the next issues reported that "the mobites" caused the closing of the Negro Sunday school in St. Louis. That edition also stated that the "health of the editor" prevented the newspaper from coming out on time. While the anti-slavery stand in these early weeks in Alton did not change, it unquestionably was milder than it had been in St. Louis. Lovejoy believed it possible to dwell less on the subject in the free state of Illinois.

* Parish, Lovejoy's middle name, was what his family called him.

The Lovejoys moved into a frame home near Second and Cherry Streets in Alton. They were hoping to lead the normal life of any young married couple with a baby boy. For several months following the destruction of his press this appeared possible. Lovejoy continued to be the center of controversy — but to be the center of controversy was better than being the center of mob action.

Lovejoy's brother John, who with another brother shared Lovejoy's home, continued to be less optimistic than Elijah. Before the new press arrived from Cincinnati, John wrote to his mother: "I do not know as this place is much better [than St. Louis]. The whole country seems to be falling to pieces. But I think there will be a calm after the Presidential election is over." Even at this late date in the Lovejoy family thinking, John condemned the abolitionists. He wrote to his mother: "I am surprised that you should join their standard."

For some months Lovejoy's main occupation was getting the *Observer* operating as a successful business. The tone of the newspaper was somewhat mild, even though the stand taken on the slavery question was clear. For example, in the issue of November 3 — a year and four days before his death — perhaps the most exciting item in the *Observer* was this notice: "JOB PRINTING — We are prepared to execute this for our friends, in the best style and on the most reasonable terms."

But three weeks later an item appeared that soon would result in a more militant stand by the *Observer*. It reported a list of people in the Illinois Synod of the Presbyterian Church who promised support of the newspaper and who pledged themselves for a two-year period to take care of any financial loss Lovejoy might have. Among those who signed the pledge were Dr. Gideon Blackburn, an antislavery leader who would eventually found Blackburn College in Illinois; W. S. Gilman, the Alton businessman who had befriended

Lovejoy; and Enoch Long, a prominent Alton citizen and businessman who was among the few to stand up strongly for Lovejoy during the final days a year later.

The weeks between the November announcement and New Year's Day were not filled with any great excitement. Early in December Lovejoy was mentioned in the *Observer* as a leader in the Illinois Bible Society, which was anything but controversial.

These first months in Alton — after the first press was thrown into the river — were the only peaceful days he would have. The views he expressed may not seem too exciting or controversial to the reader today, but they were so in 1836 and 1837. Each strong stand he took brought death closer. Lovejoy was expressing intensely unpopular views, and word by word he was marching toward death.

Late in January the Lovejoy tendency to take strong stands started showing itself again. He quoted from an antislavery convention held in Ann Arbor, Mich.: "All attempts to justify slavery from the Word of God are gross perversions of its precepts and principle."

The next week he called the idea of sending the Negroes back to Africa "utterly inadequate." But he also published some letters with differing opinions.

Lovejoy took editorial recognition of a proposal to prohibit distribution of antislavery views, which, it appeared, would pass the Missouri Legislature. Lovejoy stated his opposition. He called it a threat "against a free press." At the same time he published letters from two Missouri legislators, highly critical of Lovejoy. One, Rep. Abraham Byrd, told Lovejoy: "I wish you to keep yourself out of my Sunshine." A St. Louis newspaper quoted another Missouri legislator as furious about Lovejoy's antislavery folder. He said that Lovejoy was "trying to encourage things that would end in murder."

Barely noticed in the *Observer* was the appointment of the new Illinois attorney general, a man who would play a part in Lovejoy's death in 10 months. The *Missouri Republican* had more to say about U. F. Linder, the new Illinois attorney general, than the *Observer*. The *Missouri Republican* called him "noisy" and referred indirectly to his heavy drinking, which was well known in the state capital; the *Republican* simply noted that he was not as "regular in his habits as an Attorney General is expected" to be.

Of great interest to Lovejoy was another item in the *Missouri Republican* about this same time. Eleven members of a 17-man committee of St. Louis lawyers found Judge Lawless — the man who had encouraged the mob in St. Louis — not fit to serve as a judge. They found him "unfit, by the constitution of his mind, by the intemperance of his feelings, by his impatience in the discharge of official duties." Whether Judge Lawless' actions in the McIntosh murder were at least partially responsible for the action by the St. Louis lawyers is not clear. In any event Lovejoy was pleased to see his enemy from St. Louis scolded by the lawyers of that area.

Public feeling against those who opposed slavery was mounting in Alton and all over the Southern area of the nation. In Columbia, S. C., a large public meeting passed a resolution that anyone attacking slavery should be killed. Feelings were becoming stronger everywhere.

As public opposition grew, so did Lovejoy's courage.

In the February 9 issue of the *Observer* — less than nine months before the day of his death — he took the strongest stand he had taken in Alton against slavery. "Two million and a half of our fellow creatures are groaning in bondage, crushed to the earth, deprived of rights which their Maker gave them," he wrote.

He ran a story under the title "What is Slavery?" in which he quoted an old slave as saying:

[61]

It is to have my back subjected to the cowhide or the cart whip, at the will and caprice of my master or any of his family. Every child has a right to curse or kick or cuff the old man. Not one cent of what I earn is or can be my own. It is to depart from my hut every morning, with the sickening fear that before I return at night it will be visited by the slave-driving fiend. It is to return at night and find my worst fears realized — my first-born son, denied even the privilege of bidding his father a farewell, is on his way, a chained and manacled victim, to a distant market, where human flesh is bought and sold. It is to enter my cabin, and see my wife and daughter struggling in the lustful embraces of my master, or some of his white friends, without daring to attempt their rescue; for should I open my lips to protest, a hundred lashes would be the consequence; and should I raise my hand to hit the brutal wretch, death would be the price. Above all, to be a slave is to be denied the privilege of reading the gospel of the Son of God, to have no control over my own children; to be shut out from all enjoyment in this world, and all hope in the next.

In earlier issues Lovejoy had said that slavery was a sin. Now he went one step further and said that those who don't fight slavery — which was the large majority of citizens — "are fighting against God."

Without identifying it, Lovejoy cited one city where "there are no female slaves over the age of twenty who have not been sexually violated."

His fellow ministers were a special target. He condemned those who "preach against intemperance and Sabbath breaking, against covetousness and murder, and yet pass over slavery in silence." As a minister, Lovejoy said he had the obligation to preach against slavery at "whatever risk." A minister has the duty to speak "in behalf of more than two million of my fellow beings who are not permitted to open their mouths to plead their own cause." He added:

I have lived about eight years in a slave state and except in one or two instances, I do not recall ever having heard slaveholders, whether in or out of church, criticized for neglecting or abusing their slaves. At the same time I have seen the slaves sitting out on the carriage box, through all the service, while their masters and mistresses, whom they drove to church, were worshipping with great devoutness within.

When a reader in Missouri complained about too much antislavery material in the *Observer,* Lovejoy wrote to him: "If I could hold my peace on this subject with a clear conscience, I would most assuredly do it. My course has cost me many a valued friend. But I cannot, and I am sure you do not ask or wish a Christian to connive at what he believes to be sin, for the sake of popularity." His reader, Major G. C. Sibley of Linden Wood, Mo., wrote back canceling his subscription and complaining about the terrible insults to "the many thousands of Christians who like myself entertain opinions on several subjects different from yours." Another subscriber got so worked up that he wrote wishing that "you, your press and agent, were all in hell."

In most respects, however, Lovejoy's life during these months was a normal one. He became the minister of a new Presbyterian church which was starting in another section of Alton. He had time occasionally to teach a Sunday school class at the larger church — First Presbyterian. One of his students remembered him as the first Sunday school teacher who talked more about God's love for man than about God's anger at man. The members of the church he served as a minister were mostly farmers. Lovejoy, who knew farm life from childhood on, could speak in the language they understood.

Some of the money that had been pledged by Alton citizens for the *Observer* was not coming in, and Lovejoy had no choice but to take out a loan for $400, a sizable sum in 1837. To help with the money problems, Lovejoy's wife had a few boarders who received their meals somewhat regularly at their home. One was a Lutheran minister who stayed with them during the winter. But things got so bad financially that for a short period Lovejoy had to sell clothing and hardware items door to door. He found more and more that the people who helped him were the abolitionists, those who believed in full and complete and immediate freedom for the slaves.

As he leaned more on the abolitionists for financial help for his newspaper, he became more outspoken in his stand against slavery. By March of 1837 the circulation of the *Observer* had reached 1,700, not too far from the 2,000 he said he needed to make the newspaper succeed. Most of the new subscribers were abolitionists.

This does not mean that he was in a sense "bribed" into a strong antislavery stand. He had taken that stand before he got any support from antislavery forces. He was aware, of course, through his experience with the St. Louis *Times,* the first paper he edited in St. Louis, that if he ran a noncontroversial newspaper, with no mention of slavery, he could do very well financially.

Lovejoy chose to follow his convictions, even though it meant losing money. The fact that now some antislavery people were coming more and more to his aid encouraged him and gave him time to devote to the editorial end of the newspaper instead of the business end.

When he consulted with these men who had financed the *Observer's* rebirth in Alton regarding his strong antislavery stand, they gave him their full approval. As one of his friends noted: "He was advised by Mr. Gilman to follow the dictates of his own judgment, which he accordingly did."

The future began to look brighter. But not all was sunshine; some clouds were gathering.

He continued to make enemies among the slavery supporters, the majority of citizens. He was making enemies also among the hard-drinking element with his antiliquor editorials, and there were a great many heavy drinkers in the frontier society. He was a New Englander with strange ways and a strange accent in a population that was mostly Southern in background.

On top of that, in 1837 the nation's economy was hit hard. People were out of work. The millions of dollars that the State of Illinois had been spending on internal improvements projects were disappearing. Businesses were closing.

People in Alton were not so aware of the national trend as people would be in a later day. There was no radio, no television, and no national wire services. They did know that business in Alton was getting worse and worse, that more and more people were out of work.

Rumors were spreading that this strange New Englander, Elijah Lovejoy, was partly to blame. People were talking about what could be done to stop him.

Alton soon would be as dangerous for Lovejoy as was St. Louis.

9

DANGER AND VIOLENCE

July 4, 1837, was the 61st anniversary of the signing of the Declaration of Independence.

July 4, 1837, was four months and four days before Elijah Lovejoy would die.

July 4, 1837, was a day of big celebration in Alton as it was all over the United States. In Alton there was a combination of speeches, flags, shouting, and drinking. Everybody appeared to be having a gay time — with one exception. He was in his office, where he had written an editorial:

"What bitter mockery is this. We assemble to thank God for our own freedom, and to eat and drink with joy and gladness of heart, while our feet are on the necks of nearly three millions of our fellow men. Not all our shouts of self-congratulation can drown their groans. Even that very flag of freedom that waves over their heads is formed from materials cultivated by slaves, on a soil moistened with their blood."

That was going too far!

The paper came out on Saturday, and on Tuesday night a meeting of citizens was held. A few at the meeting had been drinking heavily before the meeting started. The combination of aroused anger and heavy drinking sometimes can strike terror to a community, but in this instance the mixture resulted only in confusion. Nothing came of it except the agreement to hold another meeting the following week.

It was not the one editorial that prompted the meeting. Month by month and issue by issue Lovejoy was getting stronger and stronger in his antislavery statements.

Some of the encouragement was coming from his own family. His mother wrote to him: "God had a great work for you to do and he seems to have called you into the field of action." Lovejoy's brother Joseph sent a $50 contribution. Two other brothers, Owen and John, were living with him and doing nothing to slow down Lovejoy. As early as April Lovejoy wrote to his brother Joseph that the *Observer* "is prospering, gaining favor with man, and I hope with God." But then he added: "I know not what may be before me."

For several months Lovejoy had been hinting at the need for an Illinois antislavery society. In March he had noted that one had been formed in Pennsylvania, with "the most respectable citizens of the state" participating. Soon he noted that an "antislavery society had been formed, on an average, every day for the last two years in the United States."

In the same issue that had his plain-spoken Fourth of July editorial, Lovejoy ran an editorial titled "ILLINOIS ANTI-SLAVERY SOCIETY." In the editorial he stated: "Is it not time that such a society be formed? We would do nothing rashly, but it does seem to us that the time to form such a society has fully come. We shall hope to have a response from the friends of the slave without delay." Then he added that he already was regarded as a "fanatic" by many — and he felt that he "must become more and more vile in their eyes." He said he had "never felt enough, nor prayed enough, nor done enough in behalf of the perishing slave."

This was serving notice to a population already aroused that he was going to provide leadership in forming an antislavery society and that his stand on slavery would be stronger in the future, not weaker.

The majority of the items in his newspaper still were not on slavery. For example, he took time to note with displeasure that a theater was being built in Chicago. "It will be a long time, we are apt to think, before such an establishment will get a foothold in Alton. We build churches instead of theaters."

Conditions in cotton production and marketing were changing so that the slave was becoming more and more valuable. As the price of a slave went up, so did the desire of the slaveholder to retain the system of slavery. Opponents of slavery like Lovejoy were trying to take away a piece of "property" that was growing in value.

This made the feelings between proslavery and antislavery people even more intense. Right at the border of a slave state and a free state, Alton was caught in the middle of this feeling.

A second public meeting was held to determine what to do about Lovejoy, a meeting which the Alton *Spectator* reported as being made up of "the most respectable citizens." Those at the meeting said they were friends of the *Observer* who wanted to stop antislavery talk in the newspaper.

At this meeting there was also talk that Lovejoy had violated a pledge. When he came to Alton, they asserted, he said he was not going to make the *Observer* an abolitionist newspaper. Now he was openly and aggressively pushing the antislavery cause.

There was enough truth to the charge to convince the proslavery people and perhaps some who had no strong feelings. It was true that Lovejoy had indicated he would not have to deal so much with the subject of slavery in Illinois as he had to in Missouri. This he undoubtedly said with the genuine belief he could follow a moderate course. But at the same meeting he also made clear that he reserved his freedom to say what he wanted on any subject, this being his right as an American citizen. As he studied the matter, and as the issue became more and more a matter of national concern, Lovejoy devoted more and more space in easy-to-understand words about what he thought of slavery.

But to the proslavery crowd he was a "nigger-loving preacher who broke his word."

The meeting made clear that they were not trying to make a slave state out of the free state of Illinois. But neither were they going to tolerate antislavery talk from a man who, so they believed, had "broken his word." To let Lovejoy continue to publish would be "cowardly," the chairman of the meeting said. He was Dr. J. A. Halderman, a respected physician. His words brought cheers.

A resolution carefully drafted prior to the meeting was finally passed. It said that those at the meeting were opposed to "all violence and mobs"; however, they requested of Lovejoy "a discontinuance of the publication of his incendiary doctrines which alone have a tendency to disturb the quiet of our citizens and neighbors."

A committee of five was appointed to see Lovejoy about the resolutions that were passed. The committee decided that instead of seeing him personally, they would send a copy of the minutes of the meeting, together with a letter, asking him to reply to the letter.

If they were hoping for a meek response of agreement, they were in for a disappointment.

Lovejoy told them that he could not bow to their wishes without admitting that liberty of the press and freedom of speech was dead. After going into this in some detail he said: "Gentlemen, I have confidence you will, upon reflection, agree with me."

Of course they did not.

Lovejoy said he would be glad to print "letters to the editor" opposing his views.

It was clear that something stronger than a resolution of citizens at a public meeting would be needed to stop Lovejoy.

The mounting tension Lovejoy took in stride, but his wife could not. A sensitive person by nature, Celia Ann Lovejoy was frightened by the emotional storms that surrounded her husband. These worked on her nervous system so that she became seriously ill. When word of this spread around Alton, it was soon topped with an exciting rumor. Lovejoy, the rumor ran, had announced in the new Presbyterian Church in Alton that if his wife died he would marry a Negro. That this story was false did not slow it down. Quickly it passed throughout the area.

Late in July of 1837 Lovejoy finally identified himself completely with the abolitionists. He had slowly been moving in that direction. First he saw no great evil in slavery; then he favored returning some Negroes to Africa and freeing others gradually; now he believed in immediate freedom for all slaves, an extremely unpopular position in Alton. His editorial stated: "In respect to the subject now to be discussed, the writer confesses no one of his readers can possibly be more prejudiced, or more hostile to antislavery measures or men, than he once was." The editorial identified Lovejoy with the abolitionists and defended them. He called slavery a SIN in capital letters. He said that taking money from the work that a slave had done was robbery. Then in his editorial enthusiasm and strong feeling he said that "more than half" of those who attack abolitionists as "amalgamationists" (advocating interracial marriage) "actually practice amalgamation themselves." Lovejoy was saying that the majority of these critics had at one time or another violated Negro women. It was an overstatement, one that did not make him any friends. His editorials also noted what was undoubtedly a

[70]

fact: "Thousands hold as slaves their own sons and daughters, and brothers and sisters."

Two candidates for mayor of Alton said they did not believe Lovejoy had a right to publish his newspaper.

Early in August — shortly before the next violence — the Madison County Antislavery Society was organized in Alton. It was clear that Lovejoy, who served as organizational chairman, was responsible for getting it started.

Public opinion was mounting — and not just among the more ignorant element.

A group of 12 citizens, including 4 doctors, schemed to "tar and feather" Lovejoy and carry him through town for residents to laugh at. The idea was to make him appear so ridiculous that he would voluntarily leave the city. After carrying him through town, they would have a canoe ready at the edge of the Mississippi. They would put him adrift in the canoe. By the time he got back, the paper would be late, and the whole town would be laughing at him.

Their plan was to catch Lovejoy at night, when he was walking home. The original group of 12 was soon swelled to a much larger gathering. Lovejoy relates what happened next:

About 9 o'clock I was returning from a friend's where I had been to marry a couple. I stepped into the drug store as I came through town and got some medicine to bring home to my wife, she being very sick.

We reside more than half a mile from town. And just as I was leaving the principal street I met the mob. They did not at first recognize me, and I parted their columns for some distance, and had just reached the rear, when some of them began to suspect who I was. They immediately came after me. I did not hurry at all, believing a man in my position should not flee.

They seemed a little reluctant to come up to me, and I could hear their leaders swearing at them, and telling them to push on. By this time they began to throw clods of dirt at me and several hit, without hurting me. And now a fellow pushed up to my side armed with a club, to see for sure who it was. He then yelled out: "It's the damned Abolitionist; give him hell." Then there was another rush at me. But when they got close, they seemed to fall back again.

Finally a number of them linked themselves together arm in arm, pushed by me and wheeled in the road before me, stopping me completely. I asked why they stopped me. By this time the cry was all around me, "Damn him!" "Rail him!" "Tar and feather him!"

I had no doubt that such was to be my fate. I then said to them, "I have one request to make of you, and then you may do with me what you please." I then asked them to send one of their group to take the medicine to my wife, which I begged them to do without alarming her. This they promised to do, and sent one man to do it, who did it like they promised.

I then said to them, "You had better let me go home. You have no right to detain me. I have never injured you."

They began to curse and swear, when I added, "I am in your hands, and you must do with me whatever God permits you to do."

They consulted with each other for a few moments and then told me I could go home.

What had happened during their brief discussion was that one of the members of the group, a Southerner, said: "Boys, I can't lay my hand upon as brave a man as this."

Later that same evening two of the doctors who were part of the gathering awakened one of the local attorneys, George Davis, and asked him to represent them in case Lovejoy should sue. Lovejoy had recognized both of them, and they were temporarily frightened by the possibility of legal action against them. Lovejoy did nothing against them, however. They soon recovered from their fright and were among the leaders of the mob that killed Lovejoy less than two months after this night encounter.

Lovejoy made it home safely, but not all was quiet in Alton that night.

Early that month rumors had spread around town that a mob would invade the *Observer* office. The printers earlier had heard the rumor and brought guns to the office. On one night the guns frightened a few men away who appeared determined to do damage. A second time heavy rains dampened the attempt at mob violence. By this time Benjamin Godfrey, the leading businessman in Alton, who had helped bring Lovejoy to Alton, was sorry he had gotten involved in the whole affair. When he heard about the printers' bringing guns, he feared for the rest of the material he had in the same building. He asked them to take the guns home. This they did.

The night on which the gathering of men stopped Lovejoy, the *Observer* office was entered. The intruders probably were the same men who had stopped Lovejoy. During the few minutes of consultation with one another they had decided that instead of hurting Lovejoy, whose wife was ill, they would do the damage at the printing office.

What time of the night they entered the printing plant is not known. But they broke the printing press into pieces and then tossed it into the river.

It was the second time that this had happened in Alton. The date was August 21, 1837.

At least a part of the blame for this second destruction of the press in Alton must be placed squarely on the *Missouri Republican* of St. Louis, which had many readers in Alton. One editorial stated: "The editor of the *Observer* has merited the full measure of the community's indignation; and if he will not learn from experience, they are very likely to teach him by practice, something of the light in which the honorable

and respectable portion of the community view his conduct.
He has forfeited all claims to the protection of that or any
other community by his continued efforts to promote antislavery doctrines." Four days before the second press was
destroyed the *Missouri Republican* came out with another
editorial which all but called for mob action: "We had hoped
that our neighbors would have ejected from amongst them
that minister of mischief, the *Observer*. . . . Something must
be done in this matter, and that speedily! The good people
of Illinois must either put a stop to the efforts of those fanatics,
or expel them from their community."

As it became clearer and clearer that public opinion was
against Lovejoy, those who were well intentioned but weak
started to desert him. Ministers who quietly had been standing up for Lovejoy now tended openly to take the solid,
middle-of-the-road, Pontius Pilate approach and "washed
their hands" of the whole thing. "Both sides are wrong," they
said. Businessmen who thought the new newspaper would be
one more solid business for the city were now either hostile
or frightened into silence. The Alton *Spectator* sided with
the mob openly. The Alton *Telegraph* said they were not
going "to interfere or meddle in any way."

But by this time the *Observer* was becoming more and more
popular around the nation, and Lovejoy had gone far past
the 2,000 subscribers he said he needed to make the business
a success. He was still having his financial difficulties, however,
particularly from people who owed him money. He finally
started publishing items like the following: "Mr. Rhodolphus
Lamb of Delhi, Greene County, has left the place owing us
$1.50 and gone we know not where." At the end of a list
of such items he added: "This list will be continued if need be.
We have suffered in silence long enough." But despite these
financial difficulties the *Observer* was increasing in national
stature and popularity.

When the second press was destroyed, Lovejoy issued an appeal to his subscribers, printed by the Alton *Telegraph*, asking for $1,500 to replace the second press that had been thrown in the river.

In a very short time the money was raised, and a new press was on the way.

After the second press was destroyed, Lovejoy began to have serious doubts about what he should do. The Alton business leaders who had financed his newspaper were his special concern, because he knew that many of them were unhappy with the position in which Lovejoy had placed them. He also had friends who, though as stoutly opposed to slavery as he was, felt he had done all the good he could in Alton, and it might be wise to move on and let someone with fewer enemies continue the battle.

Lovejoy wrote a letter to his friends and the owners:

> Having learned that there is a division among you, as to the propriety of my continuing to fill the office of the editor of the Alton *Observer*, I do not hesitate a moment to submit the question to your decision. Most cheerfully will I resign my post, if in your collective wisdom, you think the cause we all profess to love will thereby be promoted.

He asked as the condition for his leaving that the debts he had accumulated should be taken care of.

There was a division of opinion as to what he should do, and he decided to continue as editor. He had asked for a unanimous vote as to what his course should be; when there was no unanimous opinion, he did what he felt duty compelled him to do — stay on as editor.

It was not an easy decision to reach, for Lovejoy sensed the intensity of the hatred toward himself. When he had made his decision to stay, the third press was on its way.

The third press arrived from Cincinnati exactly one month after the second press had been destroyed. Lovejoy was not in Alton at the time. A number of his friends gathered at the river's edge to see that it was safely taken to the Gerry and Weller warehouse. Alton's new and youthful mayor, John M. Krum, also was present. He saw the citizens protecting the press and heard a few cries of "There goes the Abolitionist press; stop it!" But no violence occurred. Throughout the incidents that occurred during these months, Mayor Krum was on the side of law and order, though never strongly enough to be effective. The mayor told Lovejoy's friends that he would see that the press was protected.

Lovejoy's friends took the mayor at his word and left the scene. Mayor Krum assigned a constable to watch at the door of the warehouse. The constable was told to watch the warehouse until near midnight. As soon as the constable left, 10 or 12 men with handkerchiefs over their faces broke into the warehouse, rolled the press — still in a crate — to the river bank, broke it into pieces, and threw it into the Mississippi. The mayor arrived at the scene before all the damage had been done and ordered them to disperse. They told Mayor Krum that they were busy and that if he wanted to stay healthy he had better go home. This he did. He reportedly stated later that he had "never witnessed a more quiet and gentlemanly mob."

Before even one copy of the *Observer* could be printed on the new press — or the press taken out of its crate — it was destroyed and thrown into the river.

Celia Ann Lovejoy was understandably almost hysterical in the midst of all this. Their little boy was sick, and now Celia Ann was in the third month of pregnancy and uncomfortably ill, though not in a serious condition. The first pregnancy had been a difficult one for her. The second one was following the same pattern.

Lovejoy himself did not feel well, and he decided to take his small family to Celia Ann's home in St. Charles, Mo., where he had an invitation from Rev. William Campbell to preach at the large Presbyterian church. Perhaps a few days of rest at St. Charles would be helpful, he thought.

Lovejoy relates what happened on Sunday:

I preached in the morning and at night. After the audience was dismissed at night, a young man came in, and passing by me, slipped the following note into my hand: "Mr. Lovejoy, be watchful as you come from church tonight. A Friend."

We received no molestation on our way, and the whole matter passed from my mind. Brother Campbell and I sat conversing for nearly an hour; Mrs. Lovejoy had gone to another room and lain down; her mother was with her, having our sick child, while an unmarried sister of Mrs. Lovejoy was in the room with Mr. Campbell and myself. The access to the rooms is by a flight of stairs. About 10 o'clock I heard a knocking at the foot of the stairs. The knocking woke up Mrs. Lovejoy and her mother, who inquired what was wanted. The answer was, "We want to see Mr. Lovejoy; is he in?" To this I answered myself, "Yes, I am here."

Two of them came into the room and grabbed me. I asked what they wanted. "We want you downstairs, damn you," was the reply. They commenced to pull me out of the house.

Not succeeding immediately, one of them began to beat me with his fists.

By this time Mrs. Lovejoy had come into the room. In doing so she had to make her way through the mob on the portico, who attempted to hinder her from coming by rudely pushing her back, and one "chivalrous" southerner actually drew his dagger on her. Her only reply was to strike him in the face with her hand, and then rushing past him, she flew to where I was, and throwing her arms around me, she boldly faced the mobites, with a fortitude and self-devotion which none but a woman and a wife ever displayed. While they were attempting with oaths and curses to drag me from the room, she was hitting them in the face with her hands, or clinging to me to aid in resisting their efforts, and telling them they must first take her before they should have her husband. Her energetic measures, seconded by those of her mother and sister, induced the assailants to let me go and leave the room.

As soon as they were gone, Mrs. Lovejoy's powers of endurance failed her and she fainted. So soon as she had recovered from her fainting she relapsed into hysterical fits, moaning and shrieking and calling upon my name alternately.

Mrs. Lovejoy's health is at all times extremely delicate, and at present peculiarly so, she being some months advanced in pregnancy. Her situation at this time was truly alarming and distressing. To add to the perplexities of the moment, I had our sick child in my arms, taken up from the floor where he had been left by his grandmother, in the hurry and alarm of the first onset of the mob.

While I was endeavoring to calm Mrs. Lovejoy's dreadfully excited mind, the mob returned, breaking into the room and rushing to the bedside, again attempting to force me from the house. The brutal wretches were totally indifferent to her heart-rending cries and shrieks — she was far too exhausted to move; and I suppose they would have succeeded in forcing me out had not my friend William M. Campbell (the Presbyterian minister) at this juncture come in and with undaunted boldness assisted me.

Others aided forcing the mob from the room, so that the house was now clear a second time. The mob did not, however, leave the yard of the house, which was full of drunken wretches uttering the most awful and soul-chilling oaths and imprecations, and swearing they would have me at all hazards.

One fellow seemed the most bent on my destruction. He did not appear to be drunk, but both in words and actions appeared almost fiendish. He was telling a story to the mobites which was just calculated to madden them. His story was that his wife had recently been violated by a Negro. This he said was all my fault, that I had instigated the Negro to do the deed. He was a ruined man, he said, and would just as soon die, but before he died he "would have my blood."

The mob now rushed up the stairs a third time, and one of them, a David Knott of St. Charles, came in with a note which required me to send them a written answer. This I at first declined, but yielding to their urgent advice, I took my pencil and wrote: "I have already taken my passage in the state to leave tomorrow morning at least by 9 o'clock." This at first seemed to pacify them. They went away, as I supposed, finally. But after having visited the taverns they returned with increased fury and violence. My friends now became thoroughly alarmed. They joined in advising me to escape should an opportunity occur.

I was at length compelled by the united entreaties of them all, and especially of my wife, to consent to do so. Accordingly, when the efforts of those below had diverted the attention of the mob for a few minutes, I left the house and went away unnoticed.

It was now about midnight. I walked about a mile to a friend's residence. He kindly furnished me with a horse; and having rested myself on the sofa an hour or two, for I was exhausted, I rode to Mr. Watson's, another friend, where I arrived about daybreak, four miles from town. Here Mrs. Lovejoy, though exhausted and utterly unfit to leave her bed, joined me in the morning, and we came home, reaching Alton about noon. We met no hindrance, though Mrs. Lovejoy was constantly alarmed with fears of pursuit from St. Charles.

On our arrival in Alton, as we were going to our house, almost the first person we met in the street was one of the very men who had first broken into our house at St. Charles. Mrs. Lovejoy instantly recognized him and at once became greatly alarmed.

There was reason for fear, since the mob in St. Charles had repeatedly declared their determination to pursue me and to take my life. One of them, the man who told the story, boasted that he was chasing me and that he had assisted in destroying my press in Alton.

When these facts were known to my friends, they thought it advisable that our house should be guarded on Monday night. Indeed this was necessary to quiet Mrs. Lovejoy's fears. Though completely exhausted from the scenes of the night before, she could not rest. Her moments of fitful slumber were continually interrupted with cries of alarm. This continued all the afternoon and evening of Monday, and I began to entertain serious fears of the consequences. As soon, however, as our friends — ten of them — arrived with arms, her fears subsided, and she sank into a comparatively silent sleep which continued through most of the night.

We have no one with us tonight, except the members of our own family. A loaded musket is standing at my bedside while my two brothers in an adjoining room have three others together with pistols, cartridges, etc. And this is the way we live in Alton.

10

PRELUDE TO DEATH

In the fall of 1837 Lovejoy traveled to Jacksonville, about
70 miles north of Alton, for a visit with his good friend, Rev.
Edward Beecher. Beecher was president of Illinois College in
Jacksonville. He was one of the most prominent men in the
state openly taking an antislavery stand. Beecher had done
much to encourage Lovejoy in the newspaper's forthright
position.

The two men discussed the calling of a state antislavery
convention in Alton. Beecher suggested that the call for the
convention should not stress slavery as the issue but rather the
right to discuss slavery. However, Lovejoy felt that Beecher
was attempting to draw fine distinctions that would make no
great difference; no one would rally to the cause of a free press
who did not also believe in freedom for human beings.

The call went out for a state antislavery convention to be
held in Alton. Obviously freedom of the press would be discussed also, particularly since the meeting was going to be
held in Alton. Lovejoy specifically directed that the meeting
should enlist the "friends of free enquiry." There were 255
names signed to the call for the convention.

Beecher felt that by limiting the meeting to those who were
opposed to slavery Lovejoy had made a mistake. He made

a trip to Alton to discuss the matter and finally convinced Lovejoy that first an attempt should be made to get all segments of the community behind the freedom of the press. From the professor's chair in Jacksonville that clearly seemed like the right thing to do. Lovejoy felt it was simply a waste of time — or worse, a method of further arousing his enemies.

Lovejoy was not in a position where he could afford to lose any more friends, and he agreed to go along with Beecher.

Beecher set a meeting for the ministers and church officials in Alton to discuss the proposed statewide meeting. Beecher told them he felt the statewide meeting should be "perfectly uncommitted" on the slavery issue; the big topic should be defense of the freedom of the press. Beecher told the meeting of church leaders that at the statewide meeting they should be present and should get "their friends to attend." Beecher then published a letter in the Alton *Telegraph* asking people interested in "free inquiry" to attend the statewide meeting. By letters and personal contact he also urged "intelligent and influential men to attend" in the hope of restoring law and order to the Alton scene.

Beecher also tried to get the state convention of Presbyterians to pass a resolution expressing unanimous opposition "against the outrages at Alton and in favor of the right of free discussion." There was a division on the question — those opposed arguing that it would violate the principle of the separation of church and state to pass such a resolution. Beecher commented: "As I was ashamed to have such resolutions pass by a divided vote, I withdrew them, though they could have been passed by a decided majority."

Lovejoy at this time was the "stated clerk" — one of the head officials — of the Presbyterian Church in the Alton area. It was an indication that those who got to know him well had a high regard for him. The fact that a small number of respectable people were encouraging him made him even more determined in his stand. Now he would never turn back. Two weeks before he died he wrote these words on a letter he had received:

I have kept a good conscience in the matter, and that more than repays me for all I have suffered or can suffer. I have sworn eternal opposition to slavery, and, by the blessing of God, I will never go back. Amen.

* * * *

While the abolitionists were preparing for their meeting — confused somewhat by Beecher's letter saying the meeting was for those who favored the right to express views on slavery — the proslavery element was not taking this quietly.

They had decided that the Colonization Society should be revived. This was the group that believed in sending the free Negroes to Africa. At one point Lovejoy himself was affiliated with a branch of the group in St. Louis.

What the proslavery people did not want to happen was to have only one meeting of respectable citizens on the subject — and they went all out in their efforts for the Colonization Society.

Secured as the main speaker was Cyrus Edwards, state senator, brother of a former Illinois governor, and himself the candidate on the Whig ticket at this time for governor of the state. The Edwards name was a highly respected one in the state and area. Political leaders would think twice before crossing the opinion of the man who seemed destined to become the next governor of Illinois.

Edwards had been a member of the colonization movement for some years, even at the time when it had been somewhat unpopular. Times had changed, however, and slaveowners now welcomed the movement. If free Negroes were sent to Africa, it was much less likely that their slaves would be encouraged to revolt — and the ghost of revolt was something almost every slaveholder feared.

Another speaker at the Colonization Society was Rev. John Mason Peck, a respected Baptist minister who had founded a small Baptist college in Alton, later known as Shurtleff College.

Still a third minister, Rev. Joel Parker of New Orleans, was listed as speaker. He had become well known for defending slavery as something the Bible insisted the country must follow. Parker had another badge of respectability: he was in Alton as the house guest of the wealthy Alton businessman Benjamin Godfrey, one of the men who had originally been helpful to Lovejoy. (In later years, Parker became president of Union Theological Seminary in New York City.)

The two chieftains in arranging all this were not prominently featured. They were Attorney General U. F. Linder of Illinois and a combination Methodist preacher-legislator-businessman, Rev. John Hogan. The two met in Vandalia, then the Illinois state capital, where they had served in the House of Representatives with a young second-term member from Sangamon County named Abraham Lincoln.

Linder was new as attorney general, having just been elected by the Illinois General Assembly. He was tall and awkward, just like Lincoln, with whom he served. Both Lincoln and Linder happened to come from the same section of Kentucky originally. Lincoln dressed poorly; Linder dressed himself like a New York banker. Linder was a clever and powerful speaker, but crude in language and not able to control his drinking habits. In Vandalia, when the Legislature was in session, he stayed in a private home with an Illinois judge, Theophilus Smith, a judge who had been indicted and who was one of the least desirable influences on early Illinois politics. Linder had more than his share of bad habits, but he was also clever, had political ambition, and felt that riding the public sentiment against the abolitionists and against Lovejoy would help his political future.

Rev. John Hogan, the other legislator who helped arrange this meeting, was politically ambitious but not as vicious as Linder. Hogan was short and red-faced, a talkative man who made friends easily. He was born in Ireland and spoke with a distinct Irish brogue.

Hogan and Linder, the two most prominent public officials in Alton, had arranged the colonization meeting, and most of the big names in the area were associated with their meeting. The only big name not included was Robert Smith, prominent local legislator and political leader who was later to be an influential member of Congress. Smith was typical of too many. As his biographer notes, he did not participate in any of "the disgraceful acts of the mob"; by "maintaining a course of masterly inactivity he avoided giving offense and came out of the troubles with prestige unimpaired." Most of the men who were right-minded and could have provided leadership were trying to maintain statesmanlike positions of neutrality rather than standing up for law and order. They were all guilty of "masterly inactivity," and history certainly cannot view them as having their "prestige unimpaired."

But even without Smith the Linder and Hogan meeting for colonization was a big success. Edwards and the other speakers denounced the "fanatics" with brilliant oratory. The crowd loved it. The people of Alton loved it.

Linder and Hogan were encouraged.

* * * *

Forty-eight hours later the Illinois Antislavery Congress officially opened its meeting.

Coming into Alton were people from other sections of Illinois, mostly the northern cities, particularly friends from Quincy, Galesburg, and Jacksonville. One of those attending was Rev. David Nelson, the antislavery minister whom Lovejoy credited for his conversion to Christianity.

[85]

It was October 26, 1837, when they met in the Presbyterian church in which Lovejoy served as pastor.

It was 12 days before Lovejoy's death.

When the antislavery forces started to gather in the church, they were astounded at whom they saw there — the leaders of the enemies of Lovejoy, including Linder and Hogan. These men had all taken advantage of Beecher's letter and general invitation which said the meeting was open to all interested in "free inquiry" — not just to the antislavery forces. Lovejoy's fears that the Beecher invitations would be abused turned out to be correct.

But it was too late to do anything about it. The meeting had to go on.

At 2 p. m. on this pleasant fall day Lovejoy called the meeting to order.

He appointed the well-known and elderly scholar Dr. Gideon Blackburn as the temporary chairman. There was no objection to that; Dr. Blackburn was not well known locally, and what little was known about him was favorable, other than the fact that he was antislavery.

Lovejoy then appointed an Alton man, one of his strong supporters, Rev. Frederick W. Graves, temporary secretary. Those who were there — supposedly to defend the right of freedom of speech — vigorously opposed the Graves appointment. Confusion and shouting followed.

Many of Lovejoy's supporters, including Winthrop Gilman, were not present. Also absent when the meeting started was Beecher. Not too long after the meeting began Beecher walked in. He had stopped overnight in Carlinville on his way down to Alton from Jacksonville, and while in Carlinville he had heard there might be trouble in connection with the meeting. Beecher describes what happened:

> I entered the house in which the convention was assembled and found a tumultuous speaker claiming seats for himself and

his friends. None of those citizens of Alton on whom I had mainly relied to unite good men and sustain the law were there. I was also informed that some of those claiming seats had already shown their views on freedom of the press; they were responsible for the destruction of the press of the *Observer*.

Lovejoy soon informed me that they were claiming seats on the basis of my notice in the Alton *Telegraph*. Lovejoy had objected to their admission because they had come in to interrupt the meeting and not to maintain the cause of a free press. At this they were highly indignant.

Beecher then suggested that first only those who believed in freedom for the slaves should be permitted to vote and participate; then if that group wanted to expand it to others who claimed to be interested in a free press and the right of free discussion, then they should be admitted also.

Immediately one of Lovejoy's bitterest opponents said that he felt all of those present could agree on the basic principles; they intended to stay and participate.

There was much shouting, with charges and countercharges, when finally the meeting was adjourned until 9 o'clock the next morning.

After this meeting broke up, Attorney General Linder gathered his friends and some curious citizens around a woodpile at the side of the church. Linder was a man with great oratorical abilities, and he used them to blast the abolitionists. The abolitionists were complaining about losing their right to freedom of speech — and yet they were trying to deny that same right to those who disagreed, Linder told the group assembled outside. In colorful language he denounced Lovejoy and all of the antislavery forces. He got carried away with his speaking abilities and soon also condemned the temperance societies which Lovejoy supported, groups opposed to drinking of alcoholic beverages. Someone shouted to the heavy-drinking Linder that after one of his recent drinking sprees he had joined a temperance society. The group laughed, and Linder was temporarily embarrassed. But he recovered quickly to change the subject to abolitionists. His final word to his friends gathered around him was that they should all be sure to be present at 9 o'clock the next morning.

That Thursday night after the meeting Lovejoy and the antislavery leaders met and discussed what to do.

They finally decided that the original letter calling for the convention would be read. Anyone who said he was for immediate freeing of the slaves and was for freedom of the press could vote or participate. This ought to make it clear who could take part, they thought.

* * * *

Dr. Blackburn opened the meeting at 9 a. m. on Friday, October 27.

That was 11 days before Lovejoy's death.

The chairman explained that only those who believed in the purposes for which the convention was called could participate. The anti-Lovejoy forces said this was fine, they were in full agreement and would take part in the convention!

This was a jolting development, for obviously they were not sincere. Lovejoy and his friends had miscalculated badly. Not honoring the sacredness of freedom, property, and life, these men would not honor the sacredness of truth.

Another small but disturbing thing happened. The trustees of the church where Lovejoy was pastor and where the meeting was being held had been frightened into passing a resolution. It said that the church could not be used unless the meeting was held open to all who wanted to participate.

The church resolution — plus the decision of the night before to admit anyone who agreed to the principles of the convention — meant that they had to go ahead, with their enemies in their midst. Among those present were the four men who would later claim "credit" for killing Lovejoy.

The first order of business was the election of officers. Dr. Blackburn was one candidate. The other was a local physician, Dr. Thomas Hope, one who had been plotting against Lovejoy and who would share the guilt for his death in less than two weeks. Blackburn was elected by a vote of 73—53.

Two secretaries were to be elected. By the time the second secretary was elected, enough of the anti-Lovejoy forces had walked into the morning meeting that they were able to elect the second secretary, William Carr, one of the crudest of the men who fought Lovejoy.

After the election of officers the chairman, Dr. Blackburn, named a committee of three to draw up resolutions that would be debated in the afternoon. Named to the committee were Linder, Beecher, and a minister who was known for being sympathetic to Lovejoy. That gave the antislavery and pro-Lovejoy forces two of the three members.

The committee obviously could not agree. During the meeting of the committee Beecher asked Linder how he could agree the day before for immediate freeing of the slaves and for freedom of the press and be against it the next day. Linder answered simply, "If I could agree yesterday, I can't today." The two who were in the majority took as part of their language portions of the Illinois constitution. They figured that Linder, as the attorney general of Illinois, could hardly be in a position of disagreeing with the constitution that he had sworn to uphold in his oath of office.

But he did. Getting ahead politically was more important to him than living up to the oath of office.

In the afternoon there were then two reports — one by Beecher for the two-man majority, one by Linder for himself in the minority. Linder's was an all-out proslavery resolution saying that slaves were property and the constitution prohibits taking away a man's property.

At one point during the meeting Linder got excited in his

oratory, moved over toward Lovejoy, and "shook his fist insultingly in the face of Lovejoy, within about two feet of him."

The afternoon meeting was crowded with people, and after much debate the proslavery resolutions were adopted, and the convention was dissolved. It was a clear victory for the proslavery forces, for it made the whole purpose of the convention meaningless.

Lovejoy's friends were afraid to meet together that night, so they met in private homes for prayer and discussion as to what should be done.

* * .* *

The next night, Saturday, October 28, 10 days before Lovejoy's death, about 30 of Lovejoy's friends met in the home of a minister, Rev. Thaddeus Hurlbut, to discuss what to do. One of those at the meeting was Enoch Long, the businessman, who had arranged to have himself deputized as a constable. He in turn deputized a number of friends he could count on. When ruffians threatened to come into Hurlbut's home and break up the meeting, Long and his friends quickly chased them away.

The mob threatened only once to attack the Hurlbut home. The rest of the time Lovejoy's friends were able to have a quiet, orderly meeting, trying to decide what the best course was for the Alton *Observer* and for opponents of slavery. The small group voted to encourage Lovejoy to continue to print the *Observer* in Alton. They also voted to start the Illinois Antislavery Society.

Otherwise it was a quiet day.

* * * *

Sunday afternoon, October 29, nine days before Lovejoy's death, the small Presbyterian church where Lovejoy was minister had Beecher as its guest speaker. The church was crowded, and the audience seemed impressed by what Beecher said on the subject of slavery. Many wanted him to speak again on the subject, and the next night, Monday, October 30, he spoke in the same church.

Everything was orderly and quiet.

This was eight days before Lovejoy's death.

That same day the *Missouri Republican* of St. Louis came out with an editorial expressing regret that Alton, "this young city, has been made the theatre of the operations of these fanatics." The editorial added hopefully: "We are well assured that the mass, the bone and sinew of the community, are totally opposed to the agitation of the subject" of slavery.

* * * *

Tuesday afternoon, October 31, one week before the new press was expected and one week before Lovejoy's death, W. S. Gilman went with Lovejoy to see the mayor. (Gilman was the courageous businessman who was standing by the cause of a free press so faithfully.) They told the mayor that the new press would be arriving soon and they wanted authority to be officially organized to defend the press if it had to be. The group might also have to defend meetings occasionally. The mayor quickly agreed that this was a wise move, and he told them he would cooperate fully.

That night the Colonization Society, the group Linder and Hogan were pushing, met and again had a distinguished list of speakers. Cyrus Edwards once more was among those, and when he finished, the Alton *Telegraph* reported, there was "cheering from every part of the house." But the Colonization Society meeting developed nothing new except to point out to the public once again that the "good people" were not on Lovejoy's side.

* * * *

Wednesday evening, November 1, six days before Lovejoy's death, Beecher spoke on slavery in the larger and older First

Presbyterian Church of Alton. Tension was mounting in Alton, and the public, sensing the excitement of the times, filled every corner in the church. The mayor himself was among those present. Beecher was a polished speaker, and hearing him speak on a subject as explosive as this one, the audience listened with quiet intensity to every word.

The stillness in the church was broken only by the carefully chosen words of the speaker — until there was a loud crash, a stone that came through a window. There was a quick shout from a man in the balcony: "To arms!"

The protective police or military force Gilman and Lovejoy had talked to the mayor about was prepared. Hidden in a house next to the church, they came out immediately when the rock was hurled, and they heard the shout. Fully armed, they quickly frightened away would-be troublemakers, and the meeting in the church continued undisturbed while armed men stood on guard outside.

When those in the church came out after the program had ended, there were some shouts from some boys gathered outside, but no violence.

Late that night a few men, perhaps drunks, came to the Lovejoy home threatening violence. Lovejoy appeared at the door with a gun, and they disappeared quickly.

* * * *

Thursday, November 2, five days before Lovejoy's death, the entire community knew that another press was on its way for Lovejoy and his *Observer*. Public opinion was mounting in intensity against Lovejoy and another press.

Even Rev. John Hogan, who with Linder had arranged the colonization meetings, feared that public opinion had reached the danger point, that there was "a terrible state of things." On Wednesday he had met Beecher and W. S. Gilman on the street, had commented on what he feared might happen, and had agreed to arrange a meeting for the next day at his store. It was to be a meeting of leading citizens to try to quiet tempers in the city, to reach a compromise.

Beecher thought it was a good idea, and so on Thursday afternoon the meeting was held.

The people who gathered for the meeting at the Hogan store were not primarily friends of Lovejoy, it became quickly apparent.

The first speaker was Hogan, who said the purpose of the meeting was to find a compromise that would halt "the present excited state of public sentiment." Hogan said he hoped for the "restoration of harmony and good fellowship" through some kind of compromise.

Beecher then spoke and presented a resolution with nine points. It started out by saying that "every citizen may freely speak, write and print on any subject." Beecher's resolution said that whether you agree with Lovejoy or not, he has a right to express his opinions, and the public and officials have the duty to protect his freedom.

That was not the kind of talk or resolution most of those present wanted to hear.

Beecher quoted from Daniel Webster and from newspapers in slave states. In supporting his proposed resolutions he attempted no defense of Lovejoy's opinions, but simply said that Lovejoy had a right to hold any opinions, whether he was right or wrong.

Beecher noted: "I had before me not an infuriated mob, but those who gloried in being thought of as the calm, thoughtful and judicious men of the area." Beecher said he felt a chill "when not a single voice was raised in behalf of principles so sound."

Attorney General Linder got up to respond to Beecher. Linder's speeches were not only powerful, they were lengthy. Linder could find nothing good in the resolutions at all.

A seven-member committee was then appointed to consider the resolutions. Of the seven members only Gilman was known as a Lovejoy supporter. Lovejoy himself did not attend.

The meeting was adjourned until 2 o'clock the next day, Friday.

That Thursday night the Colonization Society had another meeting, with Hogan and two others as the speakers, all of them bitter in their denunciation of abolitionists in general and Lovejoy and the *Observer* in particular.

Certainly nothing happened on Thursday to calm an excited public.

* * * *

Friday, November 3, four days before Lovejoy's death, Beecher, feeling very depressed from the meeting the day before, stayed in his room and prayed. He was interrupted once by Lovejoy, who came in and joined him in a prayer and then left. Beecher recalled Lovejoy's visit that morning:

> Never shall I forget the calmness of Mr. Lovejoy's mind, his sense of the presence of God, the childlike confidence with which he committed his cause to Him that heareth prayer. How he prayed especially for the best good of the community in which he dwelt! He earnestly asked God for strength that he might not betray his own cause in the hour of trial. He was perfectly cool and collected.

Friday afternoon the same group Hogan had assembled on Thursday met in the courtroom in Alton.

First, Linder offered a resolution to quiet the most effective spokesman Lovejoy's side had — Beecher. The resolution said that the meeting should be composed "exclusively of the citizens of Madison County; and that it is requested that none others shall vote or take part in the discussions of any subject that may be offered." It was obvious to everyone that this was aimed directly at Beecher, and the resolution was adopted unanimously. Lovejoy's friends were so outnumbered they did not even put up a struggle. Now their chief spokesman was silenced.

But Lovejoy himself was at this meeting.

Then the committee which was to consider the resolutions proposed by Beecher — calling for freedom of the press — reported. First of all, they rejected the Beecher resolutions. Then they introduced substitute resolutions asking Lovejoy to sever his connections with the *Observer* and to leave Alton. To soften the blow, they said this was necessary in the interest of "peace, harmony, and order" and that the resolution was not intended to reflect "in the slightest degree upon the private character or motives" of Lovejoy.

Making the report for the committee was the most prominent citizen in the county, Cyrus Edwards, state senator and Whig candidate for governor.

Gilman, the courageous businessman, immediately protested and said the group should simply support law and order and the freedoms of all citizens.

When Gilman finished speaking, Lovejoy got up. He slowly walked to the front of the room and quietly started to speak. His words are among the most moving in U. S. history.

It is proper that I should state the whole matter as I understand it, before this audience. I do not stand here to argue the question as presented by the report of the committee. My only wonder is how the chairman of that committee — for whose character I entertain great respect, though I have not had the pleasure of getting personally acquainted — could have brought himself to submit such a report.

Mr. Chairman, I do not admit that it is the business of this assembly to decide whether I shall or shall not publish a newspaper in this city. The committee has, as the lawyers say, made a wrong issue. I have the *right* to do it. I know that I have the right freely to speak and publish my sentiments, subject only to the laws of the land for the abuse of that right. This right was given me by my Maker, and is solemnly guaranteed to me by the constitution of these United States and of this state.

What I wish to know of you is whether you will protect me in the exercise of this right; or whether I am to continue to be subjected to personal indignity and outrage.

These resolutions are spoken of as a compromise — a compromise between two parties. Mr. Chairman, this is not so. There is but one party here. It is simply a question of whether the law shall be enforced, or whether the mob shall be allowed to continue to trample under their feet the rights of an innocent individual.

Mr. Chairman, what have I to compromise? If freely to forgive those who have so greatly injured me, if to pray for their temporal and eternal happiness, if still to wish for the prosperity of your city and state — despite all the indignities I have suffered in it — if this be the compromise intended, then I do willingly make it. My rights have been shamefully, wickedly outraged; this I know, and feel, and can never forget. But I can and do freely forgive those who have done it.

But if by compromise is meant that I should cease from doing my duty, I cannot make it. And the reason is that I fear God more than I fear man. Think not that I would lightly go contrary to public sentiment around me. The good opinion of my fellow men is dear to me, and I would sacrifice anything but principle to obtain their good wishes; but when you ask me to surrender this, you ask for more than I can give — more than I dare give.

My brethren and I think that God has placed upon me the responsibility of maintaining my ground here; and, Mr. Chairman, I am determined to do that. Voices come to me from Pennsylvania — yes, also from Kentucky, from Mississippi, from Missouri — calling upon me in the name of all that is dear in heaven or earth, to stand fast; and by the help of God, I will stand. I know I am but one and you are many. My strength would be but little against all of you. You can crush me if you will; but I shall die at my post, for I cannot and will not forsake it.

Why should I flee from Alton? Is this not a free state? When attacked by a mob at St. Louis, I came here to be at the home of freedom and of the laws. The mob has pursued me here, and why should I retreat again? Where can I be safe if not here? Have I not a right to claim the protection of the laws? Sir, the very act of retreating will encourage the mob to follow me wherever I go. No, sir, there is no way to escape the mob, but to abondon the path of duty. And that, God helping me, I will never do.

I find almost every citizen against me, but against whom has my hand been raised? I appeal to every individual present. Whom of you have I injured? Whose family have I molested? Whose business have I meddled with? If any, let him rise here and testify against me.

(A moment of silence)

No one answers.

If I have broken the law, I am not so popular in this community that it would be difficult to convict me. You have courts and judges and juries; they find nothing against me. And now you come together for the purpose of driving out an innocent man, for no cause but that he dares to think and speak as his conscience and his God dictate.

I ask you to pause and reflect. The present excitement will soon be over. The voice of conscience will at last be heard. The time will come as you review the scenes of this hour that you will be forced to say: "He was right. He was right."

In your resolution you wish to drive me away without fixing any unnecessary disgrace upon me. Sir, I reject such kindness. You cannot disgrace me. Scandal and lies have already done their worst. I have borne burdens until they rest easy on my shoulders. You may hang me, as the mob hung some gamblers in Vicksburg recently. You may burn me at the stake, as they did McIntosh at St. Louis; or you may tar and feather me, or throw me into the Mississippi, as you have often threatened to do; but you cannot disgrace me.

I — and I alone — can disgrace myself; and the deepest disgrace of all at a time like this would be to deny my Maker by forsaking His cause. He died for me; and I would be most unworthy to bear His name, should I refuse, if need be, to die for Him.

You have been told that I have a family which is dependent on me. This has been given as a reason why I should be driven off as gently as possible. It is true, Mr. Chairman, that I am a husband and father. It is this that adds the bitterest ingredient to the cup of sorrow I am called to drink. I know, sir, that in this contest I stake not only my life, but that of others also. I do not expect my wife will ever recover from the shock she received at the scenes through which she passed at St. Charles. And how was it the other night, on my return home? I found her driven to the attic, through fear of the mob which was prowling around my house. Scarcely had I entered the house before my windows were broken by stones from the mob. She was so alarmed that it was impossible for her to sleep or rest that night.

I am hunted like a bird in the mountains. I am pursued like a thief through your streets. And to the guardian power of the law I look in vain for that protection against violence which even the vilest criminal may claim.

Yet think not that I am unhappy. Think not that I regret the choice that I have made. While all around me is violence and tumult, all is peace within. An approving conscience and the rewarding smile of God is full pay for all that I endure. Yes, sir, I enjoy a peace which nothing can destroy.

I have counted the cost, and stand prepared freely to offer up my all in the service of God. Yes, sir, I am fully aware of all the sacrifices I make in here pledging myself to continue this contest to the last.

(A moment of silence)

Forgive these tears — I had not intended to shed them. They flow not for myself, but others. But I am commanded to forsake father and mother and wife and children for Jesus' sake; and as His disciple I stand prepared to do it.

Sir, I dare not flee away from Alton. It is because I fear God that I am not afraid of all who oppose me in this city. No, sir, the contest has begun here; and here it must be finished. Before God and all of you, I here pledge myself to continue — if need be, till death. If I fall, my grave shall be made in Alton.

It was a tremendously moving speech. Even some of his bitter enemies were crying when he finished. Beecher, who was in the audience, put his head on his knees and cried uncontrollably. He wrote later that never in his life had he been so overcome by emotions.

If at that moment one of the opponents had publicly switched sides, perhaps history would have been different.

One young man present, Dr. Benjamin K. Hart, said he "was on the point of rising to say something that would help the turn of the tide. But I was young then, and, as you know, have always been rather deficient in self-confidence. So I hesitated — and hesitated a moment too long."

Instead, the next speaker was the popular Hogan — minister, legislator, and businessman. He pointed out that when the apostle Paul was being threatened with death in Damascus, he did not defy the people, but had himself let down on the outside of the city wall in a basket and escaped. Lovejoy, he said, should follow the example of the apostle Paul, and not his own warped thinking.

Hogan then added that Lovejoy had broken his pledge, that he had come to Alton with the understanding that he would write less about slavery than he did in St. Louis. At this point Rev. F. W. Graves, one of Lovejoy's supporters, rose and asked Hogan in front of the group: "Didn't the editor of the *Observer* tell that first meeting that he would give up none of his rights to discuss any subject which he saw fit?"

Hogan had to admit that this was correct.

Attorney General Linder then rose and said the question was "whether the interest and feelings of the citizens of Alton should be consulted or whether we are to be dictated to by foreigners," meaning Lovejoy. He hinted that Lovejoy was insane.

Beecher said Linder's speech was "unequaled by anything I ever heard for an excited, bitter, vindictive spirit."

After his vicious but effective speech Linder introduced a resolution: "That the discussion of the doctrines of immediate abolitionism, as they have been discussed in the columns of the Alton *Observer,* would be destructive of the peace and harmony of the citizens of Alton, and that, therefore, we cannot recommend the re-establishment of that paper."

There was much discussion of that resolution, but it was finally accepted.

Shortly before the meeting adjourned, the mayor, trying to keep peace with all sides, offered a resolution that stated he was for "order, peace and constitutional law," but expressed "regret that persons and editors from abroad have seen proper to interest themselves so conspicuously in the discussion and agitation" of the slavery question. This resolution was also adopted, and then the meeting ended.

Before the final gavel sounded, closing the meeting, Lovejoy had been called "wicked," "deluded," "insane" — and much worse. At one point in the meeting a resolution was proposed that the group should support the mayor in the suppression of violence. That resolution was defeated!

Friday night word about the meeting spread quickly around Alton — that Lovejoy would not leave under any circumstances and that the leading city and state officials did not seem to frown on violence.

Linder was reported by one person to have said after the meeting, "Elijah Lovejoy will be killed within two weeks."

At home early that evening Lovejoy was talking with his sister, who had come from Maine to visit with her brothers. Suddenly a large brick came through the window at a speed which could have meant death. It narrowly missed both Lovejoy and his sister.

That day the *Missouri Republican*, which circulated widely in Alton, mentioned in its news columns that Lovejoy "was to receive another press in a few days."

During these days of crisis Beecher found Lovejoy calm:

I never saw him when he did not have his feelings under complete control. And I have known him intimately in the scenes of his deepest trial. Never did I hear him, even in his most unguarded hours, utter an angry, an impatient, or a vindictive word. During the days which he spent at my house a few weeks before his death, we were all struck with his uncommonly mild and gentle frame of mind. Never did I know a man who had so keen a relish for the joys of home. His inexpressible love for his son I shall never forget. Perhaps even then he thought that his son might soon be deprived of a father's care.

*　*　*　*

Saturday, November 4, three days before Lovejoy's death, was a quiet day.

Very, very quiet.

11

DEATH

An appropriate sermon for the various church services in Alton on Sunday, November 5, 1837, would have been: "If anyone says, 'I love God,' and hates his fellowman, he is a liar." (1 John 4:20)

But there is no record of any such sermon. Clergymen who could have been Good Samaritans in Alton, so far as we know, on this Sunday morning "walked by on the other side."

Sunday morning was the last time mob members and mob leaders listened quietly while someone else spoke. Seated side by side, singing hymns, were the men who would defend the new press, and the men who would murder Lovejoy.

Sunday and Monday word reached Lovejoy's friends and his enemies that the new press was aboard the *Missouri Fulton*, docked in St. Louis.

Mayor Krum met with Gilman and Lovejoy and agreed to allow the formation of a militia to defend the press. Lovejoy wanted the mayor to head it, but he declined.

Where to put the press was the next problem. At first arrangements were made to put the press, when it arrived, in the Roff hardware store, but Gilman and the others decided it would be a difficult position to defend.

Gilman finally suggested that the press be placed in the warehouse which he and Godfrey owned. It was a courageous position for Gilman to take, for in the warehouse was the city's largest collection of salable merchandise. The warehouse was a stone building separated from the river only by a wharf and a street.

The plan was to move the press quickly across the street into the stone warehouse.

On Monday officers of the *Missouri Fulton* learned that Gilman and Lovejoy's other friends did not want the press until about 3 o'clock Tuesday morning. Gilman figured that at that hour there would be much less chance for mob action against the press.

Monday night the Alton City Council met. Mayor Krum told the council that "individual citizens" had come to him believing that their property would be in danger, asking for the appointment of special constables to defend the property. The mayor's report also indicated there was threat to life, for he reported "that they believed themselves to be insecure in their persons." The mayor presented the request with the statement that he "had much reason to believe that the peace of the city would be disturbed."

After the mayor's presentation, one of the aldermen suggested a resolution that the mayor and the city council "address a note to Mr. Lovejoy and his friends, requesting them to relinquish the idea of establishing an Abolition press at this time in the city."

The city council ended taking no action at all, word of which quickly spread around the city.

Both Sunday night and Monday night a group of 10 to 15 men, armed with pistols and clubs, watched along the river front for the *Missouri Fulton* to arrive. They intended to throw the press into the river quickly.

Sunday night nothing happened.

Monday night they broke up the wait with occasional trips to a nearby tavern. But the combination of drinking and waiting for a second night was too much. Late at night they went home.

* * * *

Monday evening about 30 of the followers of Lovejoy met at Gilman's store to organize themselves into a voluntary company to protect the property and the press. They planned to spend the night in Gilman's warehouse. They were armed.

About 3 a. m. Gilman spotted the *Missouri Fulton* approaching Alton. He and a companion then went to Mayor Krum's home and awakened him, asking him to come to the wharf to suppress any violence should it arise. Krum immediately dressed and joined them, as on the previous afternoon he had promised Gilman and Lovejoy he would.

The armed men remained in the stone warehouse as the boat landed. They were stationed at "commanding points" in the warehouse so that any mob action would be met with gunfire before it could get near the press.

Gilman and the mayor walked down to the boat and watched while the boat's crew moved the crated press toward the building. As they were moving the press a horn suddenly sounded in the city. It was probably a prearranged signal to the mob leaders that the press had arrived, but at 3 a. m. the signal was unnoticed by the sleeping citizens.

The press was moved into the building with surprising ease and quiet.

Lovejoy was not present at the warehouse when all this happened. He was at his home, ready to defend the house from the frequent attacks which were made on it, and comforting his expectant wife, who was under great emotional strain.

Shortly after the press was expected to arrive, Lovejoy went into the room in his home where Beecher was sleeping and awakened him. The two men dressed quickly and walked through the dark Alton streets toward the river to see whether there had been violence. Beecher recalled that the streets were "empty and silent, and the sounds of our feet echoed from the walls as we passed along."

The silence was, of course, a good sign. They reached the warehouse when the boat was still there, while the crew and volunteer guards were lifting the heavy press to the third floor. Lovejoy and Beecher helped them.

It was a happy group that looked at the press admiringly after it was in place. There had been no mob and no fight. A horn had sounded but no one responded. The crisis appeared to be over.

The big stone warehouse seemed a safe fortress from any mob attack. This was the unanimous feeling. They decided that the total number of volunteers could be divided into small groups of six for each successive night. And for the little time that remained of this night, Lovejoy and Beecher volunteered to stand guard.

In minutes rather than hours the sun came up, and the scene Lovejoy and Beecher saw was an inspiring one: a great river by which a great fight for freedom appeared to have been won. Beecher crawled onto the roof to view the scene of the bright-red sun rising on the river and countryside. He felt that nature had never looked more beautiful and that "a bloodless battle had been gained for God and for the truth; and that Alton was redeemed from eternal shame."

Soon the sounds of business activity filled the morning air, and Lovejoy and Beecher felt it was safe to return to Lovejoy's home. The fight seemed to be over. The press was safe, and Beecher decided after consultation with Lovejoy to return to his college in Jacksonville.

Before Beecher left, he and Lovejoy went into the room where Celia Ann lay ill. The three of them had a final word of prayer together — much more final than any of them dreamed at that time. As Beecher left he told Lovejoy's wife that the "days of trial were nearly over and that more peaceful hours were soon coming."

Beecher then left the quiet home. On his way out of town he heard rumors of an attack on the warehouse, but he dismissed them as another of many tales that were a part of the local scene.

During the day word spread quickly that the press had been landed. In the taverns talk was getting rougher and rougher. Lovejoy's friends were now genuinely frightened. Gilman sent his wife and infant child out of town, and Lovejoy sent his wife to another home, near the church which he was serving as minister.

Before the sun went down a temporary military company was officially formed at Gilman's urging. They were a mixture of many interested individuals, including some young men just interested in a little excitement. It soon became apparent that there was more excitement available than they wanted. Forty-two men signed the roster for membership in the company, but only 14 were willing to stay and defend the building that night.

The men were standing in a circle when the call came for volunteers. Those who volunteered stepped forward. Several who did not volunteer were asked privately whether they would stay, but they declined. There were 30 or 40 weapons available, mostly guns borrowed from Roff's store. While most of those who volunteered understood what they were being organized for, a few apparently volunteered "to have some crackers and cheese, and to hear some good stories."

The building itself actually was two structures built next to each other and used by Gilman and Godfrey as one building. It was one block long, with doors and windows at each end but with no windows at the sides. The roofs of both structures were of wood — a fact that soon would become important. The fact that there were no windows on the sides made the building easier for a small group to defend against gunfire, but it also meant that action taken by any enemy at the side of the building could not be observed.

Early that evening Gilman and a friend went to Mayor Krum and told him they feared mob action and informed him of their preparations for possible fighting if necessary. The mayor said he believed an attack would not be made, although he did admit that people "seemed to shun me, and were very reluctant to talk with me at all." He told Gilman that the men had a right to arm and that they "would be justified in defending their property" if necessary. The mayor said that if he could help in suppressing any riot, he would be available.

* * * *

About 8 o'clock that evening Henry West was standing in the doorway of his small store when a friend of his walked past and said there was going to be a mob that night, that preparations were under way to burn the warehouse or blow it up unless the press was surrendered. The man urged West to go and tell Gilman. West went quickly. He walked into the warehouse and asked for Gilman.

"He's upstairs," West was told.

"Tell him I want to see him," West replied with a tone of urgency. "It's important."

West then told Gilman the rumors around town. Gilman replied: "I have thought this matter over seriously. I will not give up the press. If necessary, I will defend this property at the risk of my life."

West was excited and didn't know what to do. He went to his store but decided to return to the warehouse. On the way back to the warehouse he met Dr. Horace Beal. West asked Dr. Beal to use his influence to stop the mob and get them to disperse. Dr. Beal declined, saying he would have nothing to do with dispersing the mob.

West returned to the warehouse and went upstairs. Shortly after he went inside, a large stone hit one of the doors.

It was the first sign that the mob had come.

* * * *

Early Tuesday morning — shortly after word spread around Alton that the press had arrived — Attorney General Usher F. Linder left town, giving legal business in nearby Greene County as the reason. As attorney general he could have postponed such business easily, but he preferred being gone.

Linder knew that there might be mob action. His actions had made it clear that there would probably not be any prosecution if the laws were violated against Lovejoy and his *Observer*.

People knew that Linder was sympathetic to the mob, not to Lovejoy.

Shortly after he heard the report about the press arriving, Linder left Alton. In that way no one could accuse him of being guilty if something happened. He obviously hoped something would happen. * * * *

Before the mob arrived, Edward Keating, whose law partner was Linder and whose office was near the warehouse, stopped to visit the defenders. "Each man whom I saw, except Gilman, had a gun," he reported. "The doors were not blockaded and I was astonished at the little preparation for defense I saw."

The visitor returned later and noted one other man in the group of defenders, a Mr. Noble, who had no gun and who stated that he did not believe in the use of arms. He believed in the freedom of the press, and so he joined the group in this dangerous position.

Keating was confident there would be mob action and violence.

He left the warehouse and went to Mayor Krum's office.

A few minutes later another man stopped at the warehouse. Gilman advised him to get away from the entrance if he did not want to get hurt. * * * *

One of the favorite drinking spots in Alton was called the Tontine. People drinking there that Tuesday night were getting angrier and angrier about the new press of Lovejoy which had safely landed. The angrier they became, the more they drank — and the more they drank, the angrier they became.

William Carr, whom the anti-Lovejoy group had selected as one of the two secretaries at one of the "compromise" meetings the previous week, was one of those in the Tontine. Carrying liquor to those gathered there, he urged action against the press.

Soon they left the Tontine, formed a line, and headed for the warehouse. As the small group marched toward the warehouse their numbers grew. Some who came along were only curious; others wanted entertainment and were always ready for a good fight; others were genuinely angry.

At first only a few of them had guns. Most had clubs or sticks. Some had stones. The streets had just been covered with rock, and there were plenty of large stones available.

Before long about 150 shouting, stone-throwing men were at the side of the warehouse.

Later the crowd grew much larger, but among the 150 gathered there in this early part of the evening were most of the men who had attended the meetings the previous week, who had claimed to be "friends of free inquiry."

Eventually there were 50 to 80 armed men in the crowd.

As the mob gathered, Gilman — through an opening in an upper-story door — came out boldly in front of them on this clear moonlit night and asked them why they had "come at such an unusual hour to create a disturbance?" Gilman added that he felt it his duty to defend his property and that he

would do it with his life if he had to. Gilman repeated these
words several times in the course of the evening.

Lovejoy was in the warehouse while all this was happening,
but because of the intense hatred for Lovejoy it was believed
wiser to let Gilman, the highly respected Alton merchant, be
the spokesman for the group.

After Gilman spoke to the mob — only six to eight feet from
the building — William Carr shouted back that they did not
want to injure Gilman or his property, but they intended to
get the press — and they would do it at the risk of their lives.

It was a tense scene, each spokesman stating that he would
prefer death to allowing the other group to have its way.

After Carr spoke, a pistol was suddenly pointed at Gilman,
and Gilman hastily withdrew inside the building.

A barrage of stones now broke almost every window in the
building. Some in the mob, taking the whole affair as a big
entertainment, were doing nothing more than blowing some
tin horns they had secured somewhere. Reuben Gerry, one
of the men inside the warehouse, spotted some large earthen-
ware pots and jars and started throwing them at the mob.
The noise of the stones hitting against the building and breaking windows, plus the noise of the horns and of the pots,
made it difficult to tell what happened next. The accounts
vary. But apparently two or three rifle shots and a pistol shot
were fired at the building. While some were shooting and
throwing stones, others were ramming at one of the doors,
trying to break it open.

There was one shot back from the group in the warehouse.
Gilman asked: "Who fired?"

"I did," one of the men responded. Then two or three more
shots were fired.

Before the firing started, one of the several men who went
in and out of the warehouse suggested scaring the mob away
by firing over their heads. Lovejoy, however, advised that

they "must not waste a shot." When the few shots were fired, it was apparent that the assailants meant business. So did the defendants. They fired back, and one of the men in the mob was hit. Struck was Lyman Bishop, a youthful carpenter, who had recently moved into the Alton area from Genesee County, New York. That afternoon he had boasted that he was going to help get the abolitionists. The bullet passed from his shoulder through his hip.

Dr. Beal, who was part of the mob, examined him quickly and said he did not think it was too serious. Bishop was taken quickly to the office of one of the local doctors, Doctor Hart; he was the only physician in Alton sympathetic to Lovejoy. One of the observers noted: "They took Bishop as they might have carried a hog, one by each limb." On the way the men carrying him met Mayor Krum. He asked whether anyone had been hurt.

"One of our men was shot," came the reply.

"Is he badly hurt?" the mayor asked.

"We don't think so," was the reply.

The mayor was on his way to the scene of action. When he got there, he found the mob pulled back, temporarily frightened by the wounding of Bishop. Mayor Krum approached the mob and urged them to scatter and go home. As he spoke the crowd around him grew larger, and the mayor "used all the means in his power to get them to disperse." He made no impression on them. When it was clear that they would not go home, he asked them what they intended to do.

They said they were determined to get the press. Someone shouted that the mayor should go into the warehouse and tell those inside that the press was all they wanted. They agreed that if the mayor would do that, they would retire while he negotiated.

The mayor went into the warehouse with two other men. He told Gilman what the mob wanted, adding that probably he could control them when he went back out. Hoping that the mob's anger would die down, he stayed in the warehouse longer than was expected. While he was in the warehouse he visited with Lovejoy and the others and told them that they were justified in shooting to protect their property.

One of the two men who accompanied the mayor into the warehouse reported that those inside appeared "firm, cool and collected."

While the mayor was in the warehouse, the members of the mob were not going home; they were drinking. And word of the excitement plus the noise attracted more people to the area.

One man, Solomon Morgan, had been drinking heavily and was now running around barefooted, shouting in such a way that people on both sides thought he "seemed crazy." He was the noisiest man of the evening, shouting and urging everyone to action. When the mayor tried to tone him down, the crazed drunk asked the mayor whether he wanted his daughter to marry a Negro. Morgan threatened to kill another man if he did not join the mob.

Suddenly word reached the mob that Bishop had died. His death occurred about 30 minutes after he had been wounded.

That added heat to an already burning hatred, and when the mayor came out of the building, the mob was back — with a ladder.

Mayor Krum told them of the dangers they were in, the laws they were violating, and the possible punishment for breaking those laws. But the mob was not moved, for in their midst were many of the community's outstanding men, including three physicians: Dr. Beal, Dr. James Jennings, and Dr. Thomas Hope.

Someone yelled at the mayor: "Get out of the way and go home." Others shouted agreement. One started swearing at him. Whiskey was being passed around freely.

While the mayor talked, a ladder was being raised against the wall of the building under the direction and orders of Dr. Hope. As Mayor Krum spoke, rifles began to fire, and one shot went through the mayor's hat.

One ladder was not tall enough to do the job; two ladders were tied together and placed on the side of the building where there were no windows or doors. A youth known only as "Okeh" was persuaded to go up the ladder with the flame to light the roof. As Okeh started up the ladder, one brave spectator saw what was happening and started to go up the ladder after him to put out the flame. A few shots were fired at the would-be fire fighter, and he quickly disappeared. But it turned out that getting the wooden roof to start burning was not a simple task. It took longer than the boy or his followers thought, and as they watched him try to set it on fire, three or four volunteers from the inside, Lovejoy among them, came out into the open, pushed the ladder over, and shot at those responsible.

This happened so quickly that the mob was able to fire only a few wild shots. One shot narrowly missed killing the youth, grazing the side of his head. He experienced a sudden and bruising drop to the ground.

One of the defenders commented later: "The thought never entered our minds that the mob was as bad as it turned out to be; and therefore we did not prepare as we ought to have done."

There soon were more shouts from the mob, and even from some of the spectators anxious for excitement: "Fire the house!" "Burn them out!" "Shoot every abolitionist in the building if they try to escape!"

Another mob volunteer was then secured for the job of taking the flame up the ladder. He was assured that he would be covered. Two of the men covering for him were Dr. Beal and Dr. Jennings, hidden with rifles behind a woodpile.

James Rock was the volunteer for the job. He already had several drinks and was outlandishly dressed in top hat and tails — and a rifle. He was making a big party of it that night!

While all this was going on, Mrs. Frederick Graves, sickly, small, and very thin, the wife of one of Lovejoy's good friends, did not know what to do while the attack was being made. Her husband was out of town. Rather than do nothing she went to the Presbyterian church where her husband was minister and started ringing the church bells. It was the only church in Alton that had church bells. During the entire final period of gunfire and attempts on life the bells of the local Presbyterian church were ringing.

Unfortunately the ringing of the bells brought a few more additions to the mob, more curious spectators who simply wanted to see a show — but no one courageous enough to lend any assistance to those in the warehouse, no one so courageous as that minister's wife.

At one point City Judge William Martin — according to his assertion after the tragedy — went among the spectators to the events trying to get help to stop things. He reported, "I found no one who was willing to assist in the suppression of the mob."

Somewhere in the course of the evening, 15-year-old Joseph Brown (later mayor of St. Louis) slipped into the building with some supplies, particularly bullets. When he entered, Lovejoy was in the center of the group that was discussing the situation. Some were in favor of surrendering the press rather than shed more blood. But Lovejoy was firm, and with a voice that was shaking with emotion, he told them: "We must fight it out, if necessary, to the bitter end. I for one, am willing and ready to lay down my life."

When the second attempt to set the building on fire was started, this time by James Rock, those inside knew that they must expose themselves again and go out to push the ladder over. Lovejoy was once more a volunteer. Also volunteering were Royal Weller and perhaps Amos Roff.

The big difference in this second attempt to start flames on the wooden roof — by putting burning pitch on it — was that this time the mob leaders knew what to expect from those on the inside. The two doctors were stationed and armed behind the woodpile.

Lovejoy and Weller came out to stop the threat of fire once more when rifles cracked.

Weller was wounded.

Lovejoy was hit by five shots. He managed to get inside again and up a flight of stairs. He fell down and said simply, "My God, I am shot!" He died immediately. He suffered three shots in the chest, one in the abdomen, and one in the left arm.

Someone inside yelled to the mob — perhaps in the hope of sending them home: "They have murdered Elijah Lovejoy!"

There was a tremendous "yell of exultation which shook the very heavens" from the mob outside.

The roof of the building was now on fire, and the defenders were quickly advised to flee. Two leaders in the community knocked on the door. They said the mob leaders had assured them that if the defenders would leave the building and let the mob have the press, they would not be harmed. Those inside — demoralized by the death of Lovejoy, and with the roof burning over their heads — had no choice. One of the defenders wanted to stay and fight it out to death, but he was quickly outvoted. As the defenders fled, the mob did not keep its word; more than a hundred shots were fired at the men running for safety. Amazingly no one was hit.

Two brave men stayed behind. One was Thaddeus Hurlbut, Lovejoy's editorial helper, who was also a minister. He guarded the body of Lovejoy. The other was Weller, the man who was wounded at the same time Lovejoy was killed. When one of the physicians in the mob, Dr. Hope, volunteered to remove the shot from Weller's leg, the wounded man refused to allow him to do it. Weller said he would rather die. A few minutes later George Whitney, a local druggist, came up and found Weller seated on a chair. Applying a tourniquet on Weller, he saved his life.

Some men in the mob now were putting out the fire, while others were breaking up the press and throwing it into the river. One observer noted that they were going at the press in an "orderly and quiet sort of way" and that they appeared to be thoroughly enjoying their work. As they were methodically destroying the press, one of the men, Dr. Beal, warned: "Now, boys, we've got to stick together. If any one of us is arrested, we must come to the rescue." Later that evening Dr. Beal threatened to kill every abolitionist in the city. Dr. Beal, "in pretty good spirits" the whole evening, was enjoying himself immensely.

The curious started to move up to where Lovejoy's body lay, guarded by Hurlbut. When they approached, he said: "Come in, men. Come in." He was alone with the Lovejoy body and the wounded Weller. When they came in, Hurlbut suddenly jerked away the handkerchief that was covering Lovejoy's face, pointed to Lovejoy's body, and said to the mob members, "See your work, brave men!" They fled immediately.

It was all over at about 2 a. m.

* * * *

Lovejoy's two brothers, alone and armed, were standing guard at his home. Lovejoy's wife, Celia Ann, had been taken to another home for reasons of safety. The first disquieting news that reached them was the return of Lovejoy's horse, with no one riding it.

Lovejoy's body was taken home the next morning by a few brave friends. There were cheers and a few crude shouts as the body was carried through the streets. Dr. Hope, a medical partner of Dr. Beal, shouted at those taking the body home: "I would like to kill every damned abolitionist fanatic in town!"

Dr. Beal danced a little marching jig ahead of the horse that was pulling the Lovejoy body. He pretended to be playing an instrument, and to the delight of the spectators watching the scene he said, "If I had a fife, I would play a dead march for him!"

Lovejoy was brought home. The next day he was quietly buried. His brothers reported that he "looked perfectly natural, but a little paler than usual, and a smile still resting upon his lips." Burial was in a field near his home. Only a few courageous friends gathered. It was raining and muddy. For fear of further mob action there was only a brief prayer and no further service or ceremony.

Lovejoy was buried on his 35th birthday.

Celia Ann Lovejoy, already seriously ill, was stunned by the news and unable to witness the simple burial. She was now a widow at the age of 24.

The ground on the grave had not settled when legal action was started.

Lovejoy's death was tragic; what happened at the trial was both tragic and unbelievable.

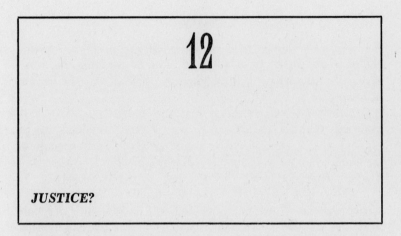

12

JUSTICE?

There is no stranger twist to the entire Lovejoy story than the trials which followed, and the fate of the men who killed Lovejoy is another weird climax to this struggle for freedom.

The first man to be tried was Winthrop S. Gilman, the man who defended his property and tried to resist the mob that killed Lovejoy. The charge: starting a riot.

The most important prosecuting attorney was Usher P. Linder, Attorney General of the State of Illinois, who was supposed to uphold the laws of the state and who himself was partially responsible for Lovejoy's death because of his encouragement of lawless elements in Alton.

Eleven others were also forced by the government to stand trial for starting a riot — all of them men who had been in the warehouse with Lovejoy.

The charge by the government against Gilman and the others said that they "unlawfully, riotously . . . and in a violent and tumultuous manner, resisted and opposed an attempt to break up and destroy a printing press."

Maximum penalty was $200 and six months in prison.

There were three attorneys for the government, three for the defendants.

It was clear from Linder's questioning that he was trying to make the issue the fact that the press would be used to fight slavery — when as attorney general he should have been defending any citizen's right to express whatever views he wanted.

For example, one of the questions Linder addressed to Mayor Krum, who was on the witness stand, was: "Did Mr. Gilman ever tell you what principles that press was intended to advocate?"

Linder and the other prosecuting attorneys called Gilman and the other defenders "fanatics" who should be punished.

Linder, in summing up the arguments to the jury, started out by saying that either Gilman and the others were guilty — or the people, including the jurors, were guilty, who tried to destroy the press. Clearly he was appealing to the juror's desire to have "the other man" guilty.

He said the purpose of the press was to promote "fiendish doctrines"; he talked about "this damning doctrine of Abolition."

Linder said that the fact that they went to the mayor for advice showed that they knew they were wrong: "A man who is conscious that he is acting from right impulses wants no advice; he acts from his own honest convictions."

But Linder's main argument was essentially an attack on the freedom of the press. Linder stated with powerful oratory:

> They talk of being friends to good order; lovers of law. Have they not taken the law into their own hands, and violated the laws of man and of God in depriving man of life? And for what? For a press! A printing press! A press brought here to teach the slave rebellion; to excite the slaves to war; to preach murder in the name of religion; to strike dismay in the hearts of people, and spread desolation over the face of this

land. Society honors good order more than such a press, sets higher value upon the lives of its citizens than upon a thousand such presses. I might picture for you the Negro, his passions excited by the doctrines intended to have been furthered by that press. You might just as well place yourselves in the fangs of a wild beast. I might portray to you the scenes which would exist in our neighbor states from the influence of that press: The father aroused to see the last gasp of his dying child, as it lies in its cradle, weltering in its own blood; and the husband, awakened from his last sleep by the shrieks of his wife, as she is brained to the earth. I might paint to you a picture which would cause the devil to start back with fright — and still fall short of the awful reality which would be caused by the doctrines which this press was intended to promote.

All of this caused by a printing press whose editor would say that he was opposed to slavery!

But the Linder oratory could not overcome the facts, even in Alton.

The jury deliberated only 15 minutes and found Gilman "Not Guilty."

The state then dropped its charges against the others.

*   *   *   *

In some strange twist of justice the leaders of the mob were also slated for trial.

Attorney General Usher F. Linder was now the defense attorney for the mob that had killed Lovejoy and entered the Gilman warehouse.

The facts brought out were essentially the same; the issues were fought over once again.

The result was the same: "Not Guilty." Foreman of this jury was Alexander Botkin, one of the leaders of the anti-Lovejoy forces.

Despite the crimes committed in plain view of everyone not one person was fined a penny, not one person went to prison for a single day.   *   *   *   *

Attorney General Linder's bright political future was soon ended.

His heavy drinking and bad reputation due to the Lovejoy tragedy meant that now the road led downhill. He served in later years in the Illinois House of Representatives again and remained politically active, but it was a dim ending to what was considered a bright political future.

He maintained his anti-Negro attitude through life. More than 10 years after the close of the Civil War he wrote that our Government "was a white man's government, made by white men and for the benefit of the white race." He always maintained that he was "severely assailed and maligned" unjustly for the part he and John Hogan played in this whole episode. The two of them, he said, had done "all that mortal man could do to bring about peace between these hostile elements."

The facts, however, leave a different record.

*   *   *   *

Four men later claimed the "honor" of having fired the shot that killed Lovejoy.

One was James Rock, who was on the ladder and may have been carrying a pistol. He was known to be armed.

Two others were Dr. Beal and Dr. Jennings, hidden behind the woodpile with rifles pointing at the spot from which Lovejoy came.

The fourth was Dr. Hope, whose position at the time is not known, other than that he was an active participant with the mob.

Since Lovejoy suffered five wounds, it is possible that all had a part in it. When we piece all factors together, however, it seems likely that the two doctors hidden behind the woodpile were responsible.

But for three of the four mentioned here the future was not a bright one.

The panic of 1837 had already hit Alton when the news of the Lovejoy slaying spread everywhere. Alton became known as a town of lawlessness. River traffic went to St. Louis and other towns. Instead of passing St. Louis in growth, as seemed likely, Alton started losing ground. Businessmen like Gilman left Alton. Real-estate values plunged. One $25,000 piece of property was soon for sale for $2,000. Almost overnight the status of Alton changed from being almost the largest city in the Midwest to being a town which was losing its population and its economic base.

Typical of the editorial reaction to the Lovejoy slaying was the Lynn (Mass.) *Record:* "Who but a savage or cold-hearted murderer would now go to Alton? Meanness, infamy, and guilt are attached to the very name. Hereafter, when a criminal is considered too bad for any known punishment, it will be said of him: 'He ought to be banished to Alton.'"

People in the community commenced blaming the mob leaders more and more, and many of them found it convenient to leave Alton.

Dr. Jennings left town almost immediately. He was gone before the trials were held. Maybe he felt that he fired one of the fatal shots. Jennings reportedly died in a knife fight in a barroom in Vicksburg, Miss., several years later.

Dr. Beal, who was the crudest of the three doctors involved, eventually went west to join the Texas Rangers. He was later captured by the Commanche Indians and reportedly was burned alive. There was also a published story that the account of his capture by the Indians was only a coverup, that he was actually killed by his own men. Both versions were published in Illinois and Missouri. Texas, however, has no record of his service, unless a private with the doctor's name is the same person. It is possible he did medical work for the Rangers but did not join.

Rock went from prison to prison and finally cut his own throat in the Missouri penitentiary, where he was jailed for burglary and the attempted murder of a woman.

The only one of the four to weather the storm was Dr. Hope, who later became mayor of Alton. He was also in later years a candidate for Congress. What Dr. Hope became famous for, however, occurred five years later when he was a second for James Shields in a duel Shields was to have with Abraham Lincoln. The duel was to take place on an island not far from Alton, but at the last minute was called off.

When in 1858 Lincoln and Stephen A. Douglas had their famous debate in Alton, Dr. Hope, believing both were too sympathetic to the antislavery cause, opposed both of them. When Douglas got up to speak, Dr. Hope shouted a question about slavery in the territories. Douglas replied: "You will get an answer in the course of my remarks." The crowd cheered Douglas and booed Dr. Hope when he asked his question, an indication that he was no longer popular in Alton.

During the Civil War Dr. Hope was "detained for some time" in prison for his outspoken views in opposition to the Union cause.

* * * *

Lovejoy's wife remained in a state of shock for several days after the death of her husband. As soon as she was able to be up, she was moved to her parents' home at St. Charles, Mo. She was in the last months of pregnancy when Lovejoy was killed; the baby was lost.

Her mother was never pleased with her marriage to Lovejoy. Celia Ann's mother came from a slaveholding family that maintained strong feelings against the abolitionists. Four years after Lovejoy's death Celia Ann was seriously ill for about 10 weeks. She wrote: "Mother did not come near me, only three or four times. She said it was all the doings of the Abolitionists. She expected they would kill me."

Other family difficulties can be judged by the simple statement "Now insane in Illinois," on the church records of the First Presbyterian Church of St. Charles with regard to Celia Ann's sister.

From St. Charles Celia Ann Lovejoy moved with her son to Cincinnati, Ohio, where she tried running a boardinghouse. It was not a financial success, and the Ohio Antislavery Society passed a resolution to make a national appeal for funds. The printed appeal noted that she is "now in destitute circumstances and very poor health on account of her sufferings."

Later she traveled to Canada and the Pacific Coast, but maintained little contact with the movement against slavery. At least on one occasion she returned to the Midwest. She died "some years before 1881." No further details about her death are known. Before she died, she visited one of Lovejoy's friends. He reported that she "passed several days at my house, a broken-down, prematurely old person, possessed of hardly a trace of her early beauty."

One published report said that she later married Royal Weller, the man who was wounded in the leg when Lovejoy was killed. However, this does not appear probable.

Lovejoy's son, Edward, also experienced considerable difficulty. He lived in California and Nevada for a while, working for a railroad. In later life his circumstances improved.

* * * *

Lovejoy had two brothers and a sister living with him in Alton when he was killed.

When his mother heard of his death, she wrote immediately to the other three, asking: "Are you yet alive?"

She added: "Don't, my dear children, harbor any revengeful feelings toward the murderers of your dear brother."

Owen Lovejoy swore over the body of his dead brother to devote his life to the cause of freeing the slave. His immediate plans were to become an Episcopalian clergyman, but when the bishop asked him to sign a pledge not to discuss abolitionism, he refused. The Presbyterians indicated a willingness to accept him, but he eventually became a Congregational minister and a powerful foe of slavery.

One month after the tragedy Owen Lovejoy wrote to a friend: "My brother has done more dying than he could living, and horrid as was the sacrifice, all things considered I cannot regret that it was made. In a conversation we had a short time before his death, I advised him to stand firm at his post; although I did not then think that this tragic result would follow, I still think he did his duty in remaining in Alton. If called upon, I trust God I shall be willing to follow the same course."

In later years he served in Congress and was a strong supporter of Lincoln.

Prior to the Civil War, one of the Southern Congressmen tried to stop Owen Lovejoy from making an attack on slavery. Owen Lovejoy replied: "You murdered my brother 20 years ago on the banks of the Mississippi River, and I am here to vindicate his blood. You shall hear me."

* * * *

The sister who was with him became Mrs. H. L. Hammond of Evanston, Ill. Fifty-four years afterward — when she was 76 years old — she wrote about that night: "It was a shock that was before me for years."

It was a shock for the nation also.

No one thing up to that time mobilized antislavery sentiment like the death of Lovejoy.

The trials in Alton found no one guilty.

But it was clear that public opinion around the nation did not share that verdict.

13

THE NATION IS STIRRED

Those who killed Lovejoy and destroyed his printing press thought they were helping the cause of slavery.

They could not have helped the antislavery cause more!

If Lovejoy had lived and published his newspaper unmolested, he would have had an influence on his small readership, but nothing he could have done alive could have furthered his cause as much as his death.

In reality he served two causes. One was that of freeing the slaves. The other was the freedom of the press. Lovejoy became the first United States martyr to freedom of the press, and as President Herbert Hoover stated 100 years after his death: "Elijah Parish Lovejoy was killed while defending free speech and free press in the United States. Since his martyrdom no man has openly challenged free speech and free press in America."

But the immediate cause Lovejoy served was that of the antislavery movement.

Lovejoy's death rocked the nation.

Newspapers all over the country condemned the action; mass meetings were held; sermons were preached; lectures were given. Opinions expressed were not unanimous in favor of Lovejoy, but the large majority were.

It was among the greatest boosts the antislavery movement had from the Day of Independence to the outbreak of the Civil War.

Strangely, one of the few areas where there was little comment was Lovejoy's own state, Illinois. Opinion was still so divided on the slavery issue that few editors ventured to express their thoughts. (This was true even in later years. When Lincoln signed the Emancipation Proclamation, the Illinois Legislature passed a resolution condemning his action.) Two conspicuous exceptions to this silence on Lovejoy's death were the Peoria *Register* and the Galena *Gazette and Advertiser*.

The Peoria *Register's* comments are particularly interesting because it was a stout defender of slavery. "It is folly," the newspaper noted, "to connect Abolition with this tragedy. All our readers know that we have expressed ourselves as decidely against the doctrines of the Abolitionists as any press in the state. We are this moment a slaveowner, possessing that species of property in another state, and we mean to keep it. But a man may write and publish against slavery until his mind and fortune are exhausted, without any hindrance from us." The Peoria newspaper's story said that Alton had been "surrendered by her police into the hands of the mob. Brute force is stronger than the law, and the fate of the city is sealed." The Peoria *Register* charged the mob with becoming "the assassins of the character of the city. Was it for this our fathers endangered their lives? The murdered Lovejoy had done these ruffians no injury." As to the men who defended the press: "Alton is unworthy of such men. They could shake the dust from off their feet, and retire to a spot where their valor would be cherished."

The Galena (Ill.) *Gazette and Advertiser* expressed shock that Lovejoy had been shot

. . . at the hands of a lawless mob! We lack language to

express our utter hatred of this act. This, too, in a town which boasts of its morality and good order. Their boasts hereafter may be considered as those of the Pharisee. The city should be pointed at as a *whited sepulchre,* filled with *dead men's bones.* Lovejoy behaved as became a hero and a man. He was only exercising the right of citizenship on a subject on which men honestly differ. To those who deny this, we have only to say that we boast that ours is a land of *liberty,* and yet *slavery* is the only thing which must not be condemned!

The Galena newspaper was also critical of the other papers of the state for not standing up and condemning the mob violence as they should have done. It was particularly critical of the newspapers in St. Louis and Alton.

They must have anticipated violence and it is our belief that had a single one of those papers sternly, firmly, yet soberly depicted the enormity of violence, the blood of Mr. Lovejoy never would have "cried from the ground." The Alton *Telegraph,* for instance, has spoken against using violence, but in words so softly that they only seemed an incentive. These remarks will apply with still greater force to the *Missouri Republican.* One of the editors of each of these papers were members of the same religious society with Mr. Lovejoy, and together partook of the same sacrament of the Supper of the Lord. The settlement of their account is with their God, not with us.

The next issue of the Galena newspaper indicated that their strong remarks met with considerable opposition among the people. To the credit of the newspaper it did not back down on its stand.

But if the Illinois newspapers were generally silent, around the country they were not. Here are a few typical comments:

Philadelphia Observer: "Lovejoy's death has called forth from every part of the land a burst of indignation which has not had its parallel in this country since the battle of Lexington, 1775. The strongest expressions of disapproval are from the slaveholding states. With a large list of southern papers before us, we find not one attempt at a defense for the murderous outrage."

National Gazette: "We shall become the pitiable and despised laughing stock of the world if such desperate acts of bloody tyranny find the support of Americans."

New York Journal of Commerce: "The enemies of Abolition must be very stupid indeed if they expect to put down Abolition in this free country by mob violence."

Boston Daily Advocate: "Let his memory be embalmed. The blood of that innocent man will not sink into the ground."

Boston Atlas: "Alton has far outrun other American cities for a reputation for blood and infamy."

Columbus (Ohio) *Journal and Register:* "Alton's only course to free their city from the lasting stigma is to convict the mob leaders."

Massachusetts Spy: "Let her name (Alton) be a by-word and a reproach throughout the nation. Her hands are reeking with innocent blood."

Cincinnati Journal: "In other countries he might have been fined, perhaps imprisoned. In America he spoke in the cause of Liberty, and for this he dies."

Jeffersonville (Iowa) *Courier:* "This outrage will fly like the wind to every part of the world. We hope that every individual engaged in the late mob at Alton may be made to suffer."

New York Observer: "Personal liberty is gone, if every man must, on pain of death, do just what the multitude happens to think prudent."

New York Baptist Register: "Woe to the State of Illinois. We believe the frown of Heaven will rest upon her, and her infamy will be inscribed as with flaming capitals in the skies."

Many other newspapers could be quoted. There were a few newspapers critical of Lovejoy, but the overwhelming sentiment, in the North and in the South, was to condemn the mob. One of the few critical of Lovejoy was the *Republican* of St. Louis, the newspaper which had actually urged the citizens of Alton to do something to get rid of Lovejoy.

The *Republican* said that "the guilt of the transaction will ever rest with those who made the attempt" to establish a newspaper. The same newspaper added: "At each time no violence was shown except to demand the press." The Pittsburgh *Gazette* was heated in condemning the St. Louis newspaper. As to their statement about being no violence if they would just give up the press, the Pittsburgh *Gazette* commented: "We can tell that editor that thousands of men have been hung for highway robbery who most conscientiously could say: 'At each time no violence was shown, except to demand the traveller's money.'"

The Boston *Advocate* was among those critical of the Alton *Telegraph*. The Boston newspaper noted that the *Telegraph's* motto was: "Men should with frankness stand by their principles, and not be frightened by the number of opponents." The Boston *Advocate* commented: "Lovejoy dared to act upon it; the *Telegraph* only keeps it as a motto."

It was seven weeks later that the next issue of the Alton *Observer* came out — printed in Cincinnati. It commented simply: "'Might is right' is our modern code, and murder has become a pastime."   *   *   *   *

A number of newspapers commented that not since the Revolutionary War had the nation become so aroused over one incident.

Within weeks the membership in antislavery societies increased many times. College students were holding meetings in Ohio and Maine and in other states.

Printed sermons in historical libraries show that ministers all over the nation responded to this slaying of their fellow minister with emotional, moving appeals.

There was, of course, still a majority of the population which favored not interfering with slavery. But never had their position been challenged as it was by Lovejoy's death.

In Boston the antislavery people wanted to hold a public meeting to protest Lovejoy's death. City officials hesitated to let them use the large hall, but finally permitted a morning meeting, figuring not too many could be there in the morning.

The meeting was billed as "an expression of public sentiment in regard to the late ferocious assault on the liberty of the press at Alton."

Instead of the small crowd thousands turned out. The hall was crowded.

The meeting began in an orderly fashion. A speech was made by a leading Boston clergyman, Dr. William Ellery Channing; then a resolution condemning the Alton incidents was presented for adoption.

Suddenly the Attorney General of Massachusetts stood up. He referred to Negroes as "wild beasts" and to the mob as men who were similar to the patriots who had thrown the tea overboard in the famed Boston Tea Party. The crowd was composed both of proslavery and of antislavery people — and a great many who came just for the excitement and entertainment, which the attorney general appeared to be providing. The Massachusetts official then added that Lovejoy was a minister who was "out of place" for mixing into an issue like that of slavery and who had "died as the fool dieth."

There were cheers when he finished.

Then a young attorney in the audience rose to respond. He had not intended to, and had no prepared speech. His name was Wendell Phillips. His talk was interrupted at first with a mixture of cheers, hisses, and boos. At one point it appeared that order could not be restored. But his plea was an eloquent one. Phillips told the Attorney General of Massachusetts that when that official compared the mob to the heroes of the American Revolution, Phillips expected the "earth should have yawned and swallowed him up." By the time Wendell Phillips finished speaking he had the crowd with him, and he had become one of the new American leaders of the antislavery movement.

Thirty years later — four years after the Emancipation Proclamation of Lincoln, which brought freedom to the slaves, Phillips described Lovejoy's death as one that "stunned a drunken people into sobriety." He added: "I can never forget the quick, sharp agony of that hour which brought us the news of Lovejoy's death. We had not then fully learned the bloodthirstiness of the slave power. The gun fired at Lovejoy was like that of Sumter — it shattered a world of dreams."

Phillips concluded: "How prudently most men creep into nameless graves while now and then one or two forget themselves into immortality."

*   *   *   *

Three months after the death of Lovejoy his brother Owen was writing on stationery that had a picture of a slave being freed. Above the picture of the slave were these words: "Lovejoy, The First Martyr to American Liberty. Murdered For Asserting The Freedom Of The Press, Alton, Nov. 7, 1837."

Antislavery organizations were using the same stationery.

Two of Lovejoy's brothers also published a small book, a *Memoir*, about the martyr.

*   *   *   *

John Quincy Adams, former President of the United States, wrote later that Lovejoy's death was "a shock as of an earthquake throughout the continent."

Rev. Edward Brown relates this story of an incident at Union College in Ohio:

Prof. Laurens P. Hickok (later President of Union College) was regarded as a conservative on the question of emancipation. One afternoon in November, 1837, we heard a rapid trampling through the college halls. Soon we saw it was Prof. Hickok, who entered greatly excited. He said, "I want you all to come down to the old chapel room immediately. I have some very important news."

The room was filled with both faculty and students. Prof. Hickok had brought a paper containing an account of the murder of Lovejoy. After reading it, he proposed a meeting at the Congregational church in the village two days later.

The next day he mounted his horse and rode all over the township calling at every house and inviting the people to the meeting. At the meeting he made a most eloquent speech.

John Brown, who had sat silent in the back part of the room, rose, lifting up his right hand and saying, "Here, before God, in the presence of these witnesses, from this time I consecrate my life to the destruction of slavery!"

It was a "decision from which he never went back."

John Brown became a prominent and controversial figure in the fight over whether Kansas would be a free or a slave state, and the center of an emotional storm on the whole slavery issue.　　*　　*　　*　　*

In Belleville, Ill. — about 30 miles from Alton — a young attorney named Lyman Trumbull wrote to his father five days after the Lovejoy slaying, describing it as an

. . . awful catastrophe which has caused great excitement throughout this section of the country. Both friends and foes bear testimony to the excellence of Lovejoy's private character. His death and the manner in which he was slain will make thousands of Abolitionists, and far more than his writings would have made had he published his paper a hundred years.

This transaction is looked on here as not only a disgrace to Alton, but to the whole state. As much as I am opposed to the immediate emancipation of the slaves and to the doctrine of Abolitionism, yet had I been in Alton, I would have cheerfully marched to the rescue of Mr. Lovejoy and his property.

Lyman Trumbull, the author of this letter, later became United States Senator from Illinois and personally authored the Thirteenth Amendment to the United States Constitution, which declared the abolition of slavery "within the United States or any place subject to their jurisdiction."

*   *   *   *

At Illinois College in Jacksonville, where Beecher was president, one of the students caught up in the antislavery feeling that swept the campus after Lovejoy's murder was William Herndon. His father lived in Springfield and was a supporter of slavery. When he saw what his son was exposed to at Illinois College, he pulled him out of the school.

"But it was too late," young William Herndon wrote. "My soul had absorbed too much of what my father believed was rank poison. The murder of Lovejoy filled me with desperation."

At his father's insistence Herndon went back to Springfield. He took up the practice of law and soon was encouraging antislavery thinking in the man who would be his law partner for life.

That man was Abraham Lincoln.

*   *   *   *

In Springfield, Ill., there was silence on the Lovejoy incident, apart from the simple reporting of the event in the newspapers. There was no editorial comment.

*   *   *   *

State Representative Abraham Lincoln made a speech about "mob rule" and its dangers, but carefully avoided mentioning the name of Lovejoy. Among those responsible for the mob action were Linder, Hogan, and Edwards — all three close friends of Lincoln.

It was not the future President's most shining hour.

However, in 1863, when Lincoln signed the Emancipation Proclamation freeing the slaves, he asked that Owen Lovejoy, Elijah's brother, should be present.

*   *   *   *

The other brother who was present at the slaying, President Lincoln appointed as U. S. consul in Peru. In a letter to Lincoln written from Peru 27 years after the tragedy, John Lovejoy spoke of "the memory of my brother."

*   *   *   *

The bad reputation of Alton died slowly, much too late for the city ever to regain its prominent position in the Midwest. By the time people had forgotten the Lovejoy incident the population centers were established.

Many years later an Alton minister reported traveling through Ohio. When he told someone he was from Alton, he received the reply: "Alton! It is covered with blood!" Thirty years after Lovejoy's death one author wrote: "Up to this time the name of Alton has always brought one idea to my mind and I never hear its name or see it printed without an involuntary shudder."   *   *   *   *

For many years the grave of Lovejoy was marked by a simple pine board with the letters "E. P. L." carved onto it. Eventually even this disappeared.

Through the efforts of a citizen named Thomas Dimmock, the spot where he was buried was traced, and it was discovered that the road in the Alton City Cemetery had gone over it. Dimmock felt that Lovejoy deserved better recognition, and at his own expense he had the body removed and had a small marble tablet placed at the new grave: "Here lies Lovejoy. Spare him now that he is buried." It was written in Latin.

Largely through the promptings of Thomas Dimmock the citizens of Alton then recognized that something more appropriate should be done, and a large and suitable monument was erected in 1897.

It still stands.

POSTSCRIPT

DOES THE SPIRIT OF ELIJAH LOVEJOY STILL LIVE?

The historical importance of Lovejoy's death does not need elaboration.

But are the battles for which he fought all won?

The answer, I fear, is that they are never won. "Eternal vigilance is the price of liberty." That may sound trite, but it is true. If we view Lovejoy's life simply as an act on the stage of history — an act that we have applauded but now is finished — then this volume has had little more meaning for us than a good television "thriller."

Lovejoy's life should help us look ahead as well as to history.

A few conclusions can be ventured. They may seem obvious to the reader, but they are not obvious to many of our fellow citizens.

The people who killed Lovejoy were "middle of the road" straddlers, most of them honorable people in the community.

The men who really shot Lovejoy were not those who fired the bullets.

The people responsible for his death were all the clean, decent, honest people who stayed "neutral" between the two opposing forces, who were too timid to stand up and be counted.

There are times when decisions may be difficult and when there may be no reason to take a position.

But there are also times, like this one, when being "neutral" in a fight between right and wrong is to be on the side of the wrong. "Middle of the road" people in Germany stood silent while Hitler butchered the Jews.

From a Birmingham jail Martin Luther King wrote: "I have almost reached the regrettable conclusion that the Negro's great stumbling block in his stride toward freedom is not the White Citizens' Council or the Ku Klux Klan but the white moderate who is more devoted to 'order' than to justice, who prefers a negative peace which is the absence of tension to a positive peace which is the presence of justice."

In Alton people who said they "could see both sides to the question" did nothing and were guilty of a cowardly spinelessness that resulted in Lovejoy's death.

They aimed the guns and pulled the triggers.

There are times when right is right and wrong is wrong — when you have to stand up, even though it may be unpopular.

Lovejoy was not a perfect man.

Real heroes are not perfect.

Lovejoy believed in the forgiveness of sins, and like all of us he needed it.

Some of his statements about men who differed with his religious views are terrible, absolutely inexcusable. This happened to be a mistake that he was not able to see except perhaps in the final months of his life.

He made other mistakes — some he recognized as mistakes immediately.

It has been said thousands of times, but it can be said again, that people who won't make mistakes make the great mistake: doing nothing.

It is interesting to note that almost half of the men who were gathered in the Gilman warehouse that fatal night were businessmen, men who could lose much at the hands of an unhappy public, but men who stood up firmly for basic freedoms. For example, Winthrop Gilman, the heroic businessman who stood for freedom of the press, risked everything.

Yet I know businessmen, teachers, and preachers (Lovejoy was all three) who are even afraid to do a little thing like asking for a party primary ballot. It might "offend" someone. In the eyes of a great many people, asking for such a ballot would be a "mistake."

And as the demand for courageous action grows, the numbers who are willing to take such action shrinks.

Those who do a coward's toe dance through life may please the immediate audience, but history acclaims those who are willing to march for beliefs, even though the terrain may be rough and there may be some missteps.

Lovejoy was not a giant of a man, not by nature a "crusader." He simply had certain beliefs, stuck with them — and changed history.

Listen to what Samuel Willard, one of the men who knew Lovejoy in Alton, said: "No man seemed less fitted to stand foremost in a great struggle."

He adds: "Mr. Lovejoy was a gentle man always. His firmness was not that of passion and obstinancy, but the gentle persistence of one who felt that he was right. There was no bitterness in his heart, no venom in his tongue, no sound of fury in his voice."

It is sometimes easy, in reading the works of history which glorify — sometimes overglorify — the actions of historical figures, to forget that these are people like you and me. Some, like Thomas Jefferson, are men of outstanding ability, but most are not.

They are simply human beings who have been willing to work hard for their beliefs.

[139]

Most changes in history are not made by the giants who sweep across the pages of our history books but by people who do not seem "fitted to stand foremost in a great struggle"; they have certain beliefs and are willing patiently but firmly to support them.

Lovejoy's fight was a struggle to make his faith something more than a repetition of certain words.

Just as the organized church was responsible for crucifying Christ, Lovejoy saw the organized church failing to respond in specific ways to Christ's command to love our neighbor.

He did not say there should be no organized church.

He did say that faith must be applied to life — that you cannot sing hymns in a church while your slave is in rags outside watching your wagon.

Lovejoy wanted the church to show compassion for the oppressed.

As a Presbyterian and as a Christian, I am sure, he would have applauded seeing the chief executive of the United Presbyterian Church taken to jail in 1963 for demonstrating against segregation in a Maryland park. He would have been moved to see Pope John XXIII visiting a Roman jail. He would have sensed a kindred spirit in Martin Luther King, a clergyman who is willing to live dangerously for his faith.

The church which Lovejoy wanted to see was something more than well-placed bricks and stained-glass windows.

The suburban Christianity which hears comforting sermons about the next world, but does not wish to disturb this one, would have no ally in Elijah Lovejoy. He was forthright in speaking about the world to come, and equally forthright in saying that right here on earth the comfortable must be disturbed for the comfortless.

Lovejoy knew that the struggle for freedom was a constant one.

Lovejoy was killed in Madison County, Ill.

And Madison County is perhaps not too much different from the county and community in which you who read this live.

The author of this book happens to live in Madison County; Lovejoy's death marks not the only battle for freedom that has been lost in our county.

During World War I word was spread that Robert Prager, a coal miner from Collinsville, was a spy. Born in Dresden, Germany, he spoke only German. When a mob formed to seize him, he could not speak English to defend himself, and this completely innocent man was quickly hanged.

These two murders stand out, but there have been many less dramatic defeats.

As just one example, I could name instances in which our county and city officials were serving professional gamblers and the underworld rather than the people who elected them.

Defeats occur in every community in every state. Whether we are able to hold the number of such defeats to a minimum will determine whether the freedom for which Lovejoy died will survive.

Freedom dies a little in a community when public officials are willing to take money for votes or favors; freedom does not operate as it should when school boards and city councils hold secret meetings, keeping out the public which elected them; freedom is challenged when law enforcement officials want to stop crime by using methods that violate freedoms given to us in our constitution; freedom suffers a defeat when a teacher or a preacher or anyone in a community is not permitted to express an unpopular opinion; freedom bows out when any citizen does not have the right to walk into a restaurant for a cup of coffee.

The battle will always go on. There must be citizens who are willing to match each defeat with a victory.

Lovejoy's fight was a struggle for human dignity for the oppressed.

[141]

We are in a world filled with the oppressed.

Some lack freedom.

Some lack food.

Some are mentally retarded and treated worse than cattle.

Some lack the ability to get a job because of the color of their skin, their national background, or their religious beliefs.

This list could fill another book.

There is no scarcity of oppressed. There is only a scarcity of men with eyes clear enough to see and hearts big enough to act.

ACKNOWLEDGMENTS

Before listing some of the sources and giving a few words of appreciation, I want to make clear to the historical researcher that since this book was designed for the reading of the general public rather than as a document of historical research, certain liberties were taken in quotations. "Grog-shop" became a "tavern," for example; archaic terms and phrases were changed; punctuation was changed for readability; grammatical errors were corrected. In no instance was the intent of the original quotation changed, but the researcher who wishes to be exact should go to the source material.

The principal resources are listed in the acknowledgments which follow. To the reader who would want more reading on Lovejoy I would recommend *Elijah P. Lovejoy, Abolitionist Editor*, by Merton Dillion, published by the University of Illinois Press, and *Tide Without Turning*, by John Gill, published by the Starr King Press.

Special recognition is due the Wickett-Wiswall Collection of Lovejoy Papers in the Southwest Collection of Texas Technological College, Lubbock, Tex. Other helpful sources have been materials at the Missouri Historical Society Library, the Illinois State Historical Library, the Library of Congress, St. Louis Mercantile Library, the Huntington Library in Pasadena, Calif., the Chicago Historical Society Library, the Newberry Library of Chicago, the Colby College Library, as well as others, all supplying helpful additional details.

My wife, Jeanne, has been helpful and patient; my secretary, Mrs. Arno Ellis, did most of the typing and retyping; my mother typed the final manuscript; my father gave many helpful editorial suggestions, as did Rev. Roland H. A. Seboldt, book editor of Concordia Publishing House; two teen-age girls, Martha Bellmann and Lois Feddersen, saw to it that my language remained understandable.

[143]

Sources for the more important quotations

not indicated in the text

Chapter 1

4 Letter to father, undated, Wickett-Wiswall Collection.

5 Lovejoy to mother, letter, Sept. 24, 1824, Wickett-Wiswall Collection.

6 Father to Lovejoy, letter, July 31, 1824, Wickett-Wiswall Collection.

6 Lovejoy to father, letter, Sept. 26, 1824, Wickett-Wiswall Collection.

6 Poem. *Memoir of the Rev. Elijah P. Lovejoy*, by Joseph and Owen Lovejoy (New York: John Taylor, 1838), pp. 29—31.

8 Journal of Elijah P. Lovejoy, Lovejoy Collection, Colby College.

Chapter 2

10 Lovejoy to parents, letter, March 15, 1829, Wickett-Wiswall Collection.

10 Mother to Lovejoy, letter, April 27, 1829, Wickett-Wiswall Collection.

11 St. Louis *Beacon*, Oct. 14, 1830.

11 St. Louis *Times*, July 31, 1830.

11 Richmond *Enquirer*, quoted in *Times* of June 4, 1831.

11 Lovejoy to parents, March 15, 1829, Wickett-Wiswall Collection.

12 St. Louis *Times*, Aug. 27 and Sept. 3, 1831.

13 St. Louis *Times*, Feb. 12, 1831; Feb. 19, 1831; April 2, 1831; April 9, 1831.

13 St. Louis *Times*, Aug. 28, 1830; Oct. 2, 1830; Sept. 24, 1831.

14 Jan. 7, 1832.

15 *Illustrated Edition of the Life and Escape of Wm. Wells Brown From American Slavery* (Boston: Anti-Slavery Society, 1847), pp. 26—29.

Chapter 3

18 St. Louis *Times*, April 9, 1831.

19 Mother to Lovejoy, letter, March 19, 1832, Wickett-Wiswall Collection.

19 Father to Lovejoy, same date and source.

Chapter 4

21 Lovejoy to sister Sibyl, letter, April 24, 1832, Wickett-Wiswall Collection.

23 Lovejoy to brother Owen, letter, Aug. 26, 1833, Wickett-Wiswall Collection.

Chapter 5

24 Headings are from St. Louis *Observer,* Jan. 2, 1834.

24 *Philadelphian,* quoted in St. Louis *Observer,* Jan. 9, 1834.

25 St. Louis *Observer,* Jan. 16, 1834; Jan. 30, 1834; Jan. 30, 1834.

26 St. Louis *Observer,* Feb. 13, 1834; Nov. 13, 1834; March 6, 1834; Oct. 16, 1834.

26 St. Louis *Observer,* Oct. 16, 1834; Nov. 13, 1834.

27 St. Louis *Observer,* Nov. 6, 1834; Dec. 11, 1834; Feb. 20, 1834; May 1, 1834; Sept. 4, 1834.

28 St. Louis *Observer,* July 31, 1834; Feb. 13, 1834; Nov. 27, 1834.

29 St. Louis *Observer,* July 31, 1834.

29 Lovejoy to brother Joseph, letter, Nov. 21, 1834, Wickett-Wiswall Collection.

29 St. Louis *Observer,* Aug. 21, 1834; May 15, 1834; Aug. 21, 1834; Aug. 14, 1834; Nov. 27, 1834.

30 Lovejoy to mother, letter, *Memoir,* pp. 133 and 134.

Chapter 6

31 St. Louis *Observer,* Sept. 10, 1835.

33 Samuel G. Hart to Lovejoy, letter, Sept. 8, 1835, Wickett-Wiswall Collection.

33 St. Louis *Commercial Bulletin,* Oct. 21, 1835.

33 St. Louis *Observer,* Nov. 5, 1835.

35 Lovejoy to brother Joseph, letter, January 1836, Wickett-Wiswall Collection.

35 St. Louis *Observer,* Oct. 8, 1835.

37 Resolutions reported in St. Louis *Observer,* Nov. 5, 1835. Lovejoy quotations are from the *Observer* in the same and several succeeding issues.

38 Ibid.

Chapter 7

39 Handbill and *Missouri Republican* quoted in St. Louis *Observer*, Dec. 10, 1835.

40 Presbyterian meeting reported in St. Louis *Observer*, Dec. 3, 1835; appeal for help, Nov. 19, 1835.

40 Edward Beecher to Lovejoy, letter, Dec. 20, 1835, Wickett-Wiswall Collection.

40 Lovejoy to mother, letter, Nov. 23, 1835, Wickett-Wiswall Collection.

41 St. Louis *Observer*, Dec. 31, 1835.

41 forward: Details of murder scene from St. Louis *Observer* of May 5, 1836, and other newspapers.

45 Lincoln quotation from *Collected Works of Abraham Lincoln*, Vol. I (New Brunswick, N. J.: Rutgers University Press, 1953), pp. 108—115.

46 *Missouri Republican*, May 3, 1836.

46 St. Louis *Observer*, June 2, 1836.

47 St. Louis *Observer*, July 14, 1836.

47 *Missouri Republican*, May 26, 1836.

49 St. Louis *Observer*, July 21, 1836.

50 *Missouri Republican*, May 5, 1836.

50 St. Louis *Observer*, July 21, 1836, and May 26, 1836.

51 *Missouri Republican*, July 23, 1836.

52 *The Martyrdom of Lovejoy*, by Henry Tanner (Chicago: Fergus, 1881), pp. 89 and 90.

Chapter 8

56 "Lovejoy," an address by Thomas Dimmock, Illinois State Historical Society Library, pp. 10 and 11.

57 Alton *Telegraph*, Aug. 10, 1836.

57 John Lovejoy to mother, letter, Sept. 4, 1836, Wickett-Wiswall Collection.

58 Alton *Observer*, Sept. 8, 1836.

58 Alton *Observer*, Sept. 29, 1836.

60 Alton *Observer*, Jan. 26, 1837; Feb. 2, 1837.

61 *Missouri Republican*, Feb. 15, 1837; Feb. 7, 1837.

61 Most of quotations from Alton *Observer*, Feb. 9, 1837.

62 Alton *Observer*, Feb. 9, 1837.

63 Ibid.

63 Lovejoy to Major G. C. Sibley, letter, April 27, 1837, Missouri State Historical Society Library.

63 Major G. C. Sibley to Lovejoy, letter, June 12, 1837, Missouri State Historical Society Library.

63 Alton *Observer,* May 4, 1837.

64 *Narrative of Riots at Alton,* by Edward Beecher (Alton: George Holton, 1838), p. 20.

Chapter 9

66 Alton *Observer,* July 6, 1837.

67 Mother to Lovejoy, letter, 1837 (no date), Wickett-Wiswall Collection.

67 Lovejoy to brother Joseph, letter, April 14, 1837, Wickett-Wiswall Collection.

67 Alton *Observer,* March 9, 1837; March 16, 1837; July 6, 1837.

68 Alton *Observer,* June 22, 1837.

69 Alton *Observer,* July 20, 1837. Lovejoy printed both the proceedings of the meeting and his reply.

70 Alton *Observer,* July 20, 1837.

72 *Memoir,* pp. 232—234.

74 Alton *Telegraph,* Oct. 11, 1837.

74 Alton *Observer,* July 20, 1837.

75 Lovejoy to Lewis Tappan and others, letters, Sept. 11, 1837, Library of Congress.

80 St. Charles incident in *Memoir,* pp. 251—260.

Chapter 10

81 Beecher, op. cit., gives his account of the entire proceedings.

83 *Memoir,* p. 138.

85 "Hon. Robert Smith, forgotten Statesman of Illinois," by W. T. Norton, *Illinois State Historical Society Journal,* October 1915, p. 428.

87 Beecher, pp. 28 and 29.

90 Samuel Willard, quoted in Tanner, op. cit., p. 220.

90 Beecher, p. 32.

91 *Missouri Republican,* Oct. 30, 1837.

93 Quotation from Hogan and detailed account of the meeting in *Missouri Republican,* Nov. 10, 1837.

93 Beecher, p. 60.

94 Beecher, p. 65.

99 Lovejoy's speech is quoted in Beecher, pp. 85—91. After the meeting Lovejoy and Beecher went home together, and as accurately as possible they tried to recall what Lovejoy had said, and then wrote it down.

99 Quotations all from *Missouri Republican*, Nov. 10, 1837.

100 *Tide Without Turning*, by John Gill (Boston: Starr King Press, 1958), p. 181, quotes Linder as saying this. No source is given.

101 Beecher, pp. 141—144.

101 *Missouri Republican*, Nov. 3, 1837.

Chapter 11

105 Beecher, p. 100.

105 Beecher, pp. 101—103.

106 forward: All quotations not otherwise attributed in the remainder of this chapter are from the *Alton Trials*, referred to earlier. At the trials many of the people involved testified under oath as to what happened. Fortunately this was recorded by a court reporter.

111 Samuel Willard, quoted in Tanner, p. 226.

113 Alton *Observer*, Dec. 28, 1837; and *Sangamon Journal*, Nov. 18, 1837, quoting statement from Mayor Krum.

115 *Memoir*, p. 291.

117 *Memoir*, p. 292.

117 W. C. Quigley letter, dated Nov. 7, 1880, Illinois Historical Society Library, relates the incident at the scene of death.

Chapter 12

118 Account of trial in *Alton Trials*.

121 *Reminiscences of the Early Bench and Bar of Illinois*, by Usher F. Linder (Chicago, 1876), pp. 223 and 372.

122 Quoted in *Memoir*, p. 332.

123 Quoted in several newspapers and in *Created Equal*, by Paul Angle (Chicago: University of Chicago Press, 1958), p. 362.

123 *Centennial History of Madison County*, Vol. I, by W. T. Norton (Chicago, 1912), p. 387.

124 Celia Ann Lovejoy to Lovejoy's mother, letter, April 10, 1841, Wickett-Wiswall Collection.

124 Tanner, footnote on p. 90.

124 Lovejoy's mother to Owen, Elizabeth, and John, letter, December 1837, Wickett-Wiswall Collection.

125 Owen Lovejoy to J. G. Birney, letter, Dec. 9, 1837, Illinois State Historical Society Library.

125 "Elijah P. Lovejoy," by M. K. Whittlesey, *Magazine of Western History,* July 1887.

125 Mrs. H. L. Hammond to Thomas Dimmock, letter, June 1, 1891, Missouri State Historical Society Library.

Chapter 13

126 From program of 100th anniversary of death of Lovejoy, at Colby College.

127 Most quotations from other newspapers are from the Dec. 28, 1837, Alton *Observer.* However, almost all original sources have some. Unless otherwise indicated, it is taken from one of the publications already mentioned.

128 Galena *Gazette and Advertiser,* Galena, Ill., Nov. 18, 1837.

129 Newspaper quotations from several sources, including Tanner, pp. 168 ff., which quotes newspaper accounts.

132 Feb. 10, 1838, Owen Lovejoy used a letterhead described in the text. Wickett-Wiswall Collection.

132 Adams quoted in *Memoir,* p. 12.

133 Story related by Rev. Edward Brown, cousin of John Brown, in "Lovejoy's Influence on John Brown" by Justus Newton Brown, *Magazine of History,* September—October 1916.

134 Trumbull to father, Nov. 12, 1837, letter, quoted in *The Life of Lyman Trumbull,* by Horace White (New York: Houghton Mifflin, 1913), pp. 8—10.

134 *Herndon's Life of Lincoln,* edited by Paul Angle (New York: World Publishing Company, 1949), p. 150.

135 John Lovejoy to Lincoln, Sept. 23, 1864. Robert Todd Lincoln Collection, Library of Congress.

135 Melvin Jameson relates the incident in his small book, *Elijah Parish Lovejoy as a Christian* (Rochester, N. Y.: Wetmore & Co., 1907), p. 8.

135 Wendell Phillips is the author. He mentioned this in a letter written from Alton to the *Anti-Slavery Standard,* April 14, 1867. It was reprinted in the Alton *Evening Telegraph.*

Postscript

139 Willard, quoted in Tanner, pp. 216 and 217.

The first copy of this book was placed in the new library at the Edwardsville Campus of Southern Illinois University, located about 15 miles from the scene of Lovejoy's death and burial place. The name chosen for the library: The Elijah Parish Lovejoy Memorial Library.